COMPOSERS OF TOMORROW'S MUSIC

Also by David Ewen

Famous Instrumentalists
Famous Conductors
Famous Modern Composers
Composers for the American Musical Theatre
Richard Rodgers
Leonard Bernstein
Music for the Millions
Music Comes to America
The World of Great Composers
The Encyclopedia of the Opera
The New Book of Modern Composers
The Encyclopedia of Concert Music
The Home Book of Musical Knowledge
David Ewen Introduces Modern Music
Great Men of American Popular Song
The Life and Death of Tin Pan Alley
The Complete Book of Classical Music
The World of Twentieth-Century Music
The Story of America's Musical Theater
New Complete Book of the American Musical Theater
American Popular Songs: From the Revolutionary War to the Present
The Milton Cross New Encyclopedia of Great Composers and their
     Music (*with Milton Cross*)
George Gershwin: His Journey to Greatness

Composers
of Tomorrow's
Music

*A non-technical introduction
to the musical avant-garde movement*

by David Ewen

Illustrated with Photographs

DODD, MEAD & COMPANY

NEW YORK

ISBN 0-396-06286-5
Library of Congress Catalog Card Number: 75-136499

Printed in the United States of America
by The Cornwall Press, Inc., Cornwall, N. Y.

"Strange Things are Happening."

Introduction

When "Red" Buttons, the actor, used to have his own weekly television show a number of years ago, he used a routine as his personal trademark practically on each broadcast. From time to time he would cup his hands over his ears, cock his head to one side while his eyes sparkled with hidden laughter, and exclaim: "Strange things are happening!"

This routine invariably springs to my mind whenever I watch audiences emerging from a concert featuring avant-garde music. These audiences, too, have a gleam of hidden laughter in their eyes. They, too, mutter "Strange things are happening." They, too—figuratively at any rate—have cupped their hands over their ears.

It is true: Strange things have been happening to some of today's music. Melody has been reduced to scattered tones, sometimes even to a single tone. Neatly patterned musical structures are replaced by seemingly shapeless forms, in which the tones and sounds seem to move about aimlessly, as if in an amorphous mold. The old well-tried tools of the composer's trade—the traditional diatonic and chromatic scales, harmony, thematic development and variation, the familiar instruments, a notation that anybody who has had a musical training can readily read—appear to have been dumped into discard.

The twelve-tone composers and the serialists that followed them were bad enough in the strange new way that music was being conceived and concocted. Worse was still to come. After that we had "aleatory" music in which the composer used all sorts of methods to have his compositions created not by calculation but by chance methods—so that he himself never really knew what kind of music he was producing until it had been performed. And we had "directional" or "spatial" music, in which musical sounds converged on an audience from many different directions rather than coming to it from one—the stage. And we had music that was not music at all, but organized sounds—noises, to put it bluntly. Electronics helped open up an entirely new world of sound possibilities—on doctored magnetic tape, through computers, on synthesizers. And we had music that made a fetish of utter nonsense come from a new school of dadaists.

In these instances what was happening was outright revolution, a total and permanent break with the past, the opening up of a new, unexplored world for musical creativity.

Strange things had been happening to music in the twentieth century even before the avant-garde overturned the existing order. Today, our concert audiences are quite ready to assign importance to composers such as Igor

Stravinsky, Béla Bartók, Paul Hindemith, Dmitri Shosta-kovich, Serge Prokofiev, Arthur Honegger, William Schu-man, Samuel Barber, and Aaron Copland. Indeed, audi-ences have come to learn to enjoy the major works of these and other twentieth-century masters—even to the point of being willing to spend hard cash to purchase recordings of their compositions. But all these composers were also rebels —against the Classical and Romantic practices that had preceded them. They, too, broke the rules. Their thematic material was hardly of the melodic kind that stirred senti-ment as did the melodies of a Haydn, Mozart, Beethoven, Brahms, and Tchaikovsky. Usually the melodic lines of these modern compositions were harsh, stark, angular, with very little emotional stimulus. In addition, savage-sounding discords predominated in place of a pleasant concord of tones. Primitive rhythmic forces were released. The music of most of these moderns was often so complex that it took numerous hearings to discover the logic governing it. Yet audiences (at least a good many of them) have grown used to this kind of music as opposed to that of past eras and find a good deal of fascination and even beauty, as well as originality, in compositions which today are placed in the category of classics: for example, Stravinsky's *Petrouchka* and *The Rite of Spring;* Bartók's string quartets and his *Concerto for Orchestra;* Hindemith's symphonies and his opera, *Mathis der Maler;* Honegger's *Joan of Arc at the Stake;* Prokofiev's Fifth Symphony and Third Piano Con-certo; Shostakovich's First and Fifth Symphonies; Sir William Walton's opera *Troilus and Cressida,* Violin Con-certo, and two symphonies; Britten's operas *Peter Grimes* and *Billy Budd;* William Schuman's later symphonies and choral music; Samuel Barber's Piano Concerto and his opera *Vanessa*. (Naturally I am picking only a representative list of significant modern works; there are many, many others.) Familiarity, in short, has brought not contempt, but appreciation and understanding.

Audiences were able in time to get accustomed to and value the composers and compositions mentioned above because these composers and their music represented a process of *evolution*. However modern their approach, idiom, and techniques, these composers still used the traditional scales, instruments, structures, notation, with few and negligible exceptions. If they preferred discords to concord, if they combined contrapuntal lines of music each in a different tonality, if they made rhythm rather than melody the prime force—all this, after all, was only a new way of using old materials (harmony, counterpoint, rhythm). These composers took inherited materials and used them with liberties and independence—in fact precisely in the same way the Romantic composers before them, from Schubert on through Wagner and Mahler and Bruckner, had taken liberties with the inheritance they had received from the Classical era.

But once the avant-garde composer entered our musical life, he did not just put new wine into old bottles, as had been the case up to now. He produced a vintage all his own and poured it into entirely new vessels. As I have said before, this was revolution (not evolution) of a kind music had not experienced since the late sixteenth century when the age of polyphony was succeeded by the homophonic era.

In polyphony, music consists of choral music in which several different melodies are sung simultaneously. At that time—the fifteenth and sixteenth centuries—instrumental music occupied a comparatively insignificant role. Most often instruments served merely as accompaniment to choral compositions, although a good deal of choral music was written for unaccompanied voice (*a capella*). When on rare occasions composers did write music for instruments without human voices, here, too, they employed a polyphonic technique.

Then homophony was developed in which a single melody moved over a harmonic background. This totally new concept in the writing of music not only made possible the emergence of opera but also helped to bring instrumental music to a position of major importance. Forms such as the sonata, concerto, symphony, quartet, and overture were now developed. Major and minor scales replaced the old church modes that had previously been used for polyphonic choral music.

Such an upheaval created furor and aroused fierce opposition from those diehards who preferred clinging to old practices. The first great composer in this revolution, and the first great composer of operas, Claudio Monteverdi (1567–1643), was called a madman by the critics of his time. But in spite of the hostility of the reactionaries, the homophonic revolution could no more be stopped than you can halt a hurricane with a gesture of an upturned palm of the hand. Out of this revolution has sprung that fabulous repertory of musical masterworks that have inspired and exalted music lovers for over two centuries.

Since the 1950's, a new revolution has taken place, even more drastic than the one that replaced polyphony with homophony. (This does not mean, of course, that there have not been composers since the 1950s who still cling to the past and are pleasant and easy to listen to.) A new school of rebels forged to the front. They insisted that the technical materials previously used by the masters had become so shopworn that they were no longer serviceable. Using those older materials led merely to imitation, not to invention. Can a present-day writer of novels or plays—they argued—use the methods, the messages, and the styles of the great writers of the past? A totally new art had to spring up to express our hypertensive, turbulent, technological era. Many composers made it their business to invent such a new art. They inaugurated for music the age of "sounds" as opposed to the harmonic age.

The result was the discovery of a whole new world of sound and of musical aesthetics for which there was no precedent. No longer were the regular scales used; no longer were the elements of harmony, counterpoint, rhythm, melody the vocabulary of music; new "instruments" came into existence capable of creating sounds music had never before known; a new notation had to be devised to put these sounds on paper. In short, totally new materials had to be devised; totally new concepts had to be arrived at; totally new sounds had to be invented for a world that has undergone a greater transformation in the past quarter of a century than in any one century before this. For such a changed world the vistas of musical creativity had to be broadened. It is impossible at this time to guess what lies beyond the horizon in music; but thanks to the more successful experiments of the avant-garde composer, we are beginning to get an idea.

The avant-garde composer may be an eccentric and an original, of course, but he is also usually a profound student thoroughly trained in the music of the past, completely versed in musical literature, a thorough master of the techniques he has discarded. Most of these avant-garde composers could, if they wished, produce symphonies, concertos, and operas full of listenable melodies and pleasurable harmonies within clearly designed structures. But the avant-garde composer writes the way he does because he is driven by the same uncontrollable impulses that led Monteverdi to introduce tremolos and pizzicati (for the first time in music history) into his early seventeenth-century operas to achieve dramatic effects unknown in the music of his time; that impelled Beethoven to use discords and vague tonalities, as well as fragmentary thematic materials, in his last string quartets; that compelled Schubert to evolve an altogether new type of song (the *Lied,* or art song), while his contemporaries condemned him for his "lack of melody" (he whom we now regard as the greatest melodist the world has known!); that drove Wagner and Debussy to achieve new methods because the older ones simply failed to serve their creative aims. And in the past, as today, there were always audiences muttering that "strange things are happening," while cupping hands over ears.

Because the music of avant-garde movement is so without precedent, it has proved virtually incomprehensible to most concert and opera goers. And so most music lovers tend, so to speak, to press hands over ears when this new music gets played. What I shall try to do in this book is to remove their hands from their ears. I shall try to rid these music lovers of inherited prejudices of what music should or should not sound like. I shall introduce some of the major avant-garde composers and try to explain what it is they are aiming for.

Surely the time has come for the adult music lover to

begin to understand what the avant-garde movement in music is all about. And even more surely there is a crying need to explain this music to young sophisticated concert goers, since this new movement will be producing the music with which they will be living both in the near and in the more distant future.

Contents

PHOTOGRAPHIC SUPPLEMENT

CHARLES IVES

ARNOLD SCHOENBERG

ALBAN BERG

ANTON WEBERN

ALBERTO GINASTERA

Wide World Photos

JOHN CAGE

IGOR STRAVINSKY

United Press International Photo

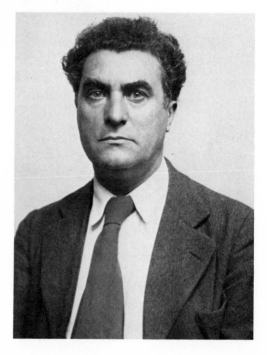

EDGARD VARESE

KARLHEINZ STOCKHAUSEN

LUCIANO BERIO

High Fidelity

YANNIS XENAKIS

Keith Holzman

MILTON BABBITT

Charlotte Till-Borchardt

PIERRE BOULEZ

LUKAS FOSS

HARRY PARTCH

Ken De Roux

I | *He was the ancestor of our*
avant-garde.

Charles Ives

(1874–1954)

At the beginning of the twentieth century there lived an
American composer who knew with finality that the established way of writing music had come to the end of a
long road. He knew that music had to change, and change
radically, if it were to continue as a vital, living force.
With a sublime disregard of what other composers of his
time were writing, and how, and with a complete disdain
of what the public of his day expected to hear and critics
stood ready to accept, he proceeded to produce new *sounds*
while adopting new procedures, new idioms, new techniques. His need to write his strange, new kind of music
was a drive he could not suppress. The old kind of music
represented to him so much dead tissue.

The name of this composer is Charles Ives. Surely he is
one of the strangest personalities music has known, and
his career is without parallel. Usually in his musical writing he was a visionary and a revolutionist. But sometimes

he was as mischievous and whimsical as a schoolboy annoy-
ing his parents. Today, more than half a century since he
put his music down on paper, many critics regard him as
possibly the greatest composer America has produced. Yet
until the closing years of his life the music world had not
the slightest idea who he was. If they knew anything about
him, they had never heard or seen any of his music. Nor
were they aware that audacities which had become common practice among the world's most famous composers
had first been perpetrated by Ives almost half a century
earlier. For during the period when all his compositions
were written, Ives lived and worked as a composer in total
obscurity. This is the way he wanted it to be.

Charles Ives wrote his music solely for his own pleasure.
By profession he was the head of a prosperous insurance
firm. For convenience, to be near his office, he and his
family occupied a brownstone house on East Seventy-fourth
Street in New York. A good deal of his success in insurance
was due to his "hardheaded common sense," as Henry
Bellamann wrote in *Musical Quarterly* before Ives gained
recognition for his music. Putting over a deal, Ives was no
"wild-eyed revolutionary inhabiting the regions of Bo-
hemia, but a normal citizen who . . . pursued his own way,
going to business in the downtown New York district." He
was practical, conservative, well trained in the handling of
his affairs. During business hours he dressed moderately
and in good taste. Looking at him across the desk in his
insurance office, you would have found it impossible to dis-
tinguish his superficial characteristics from those of other
highly successful New York businessmen. Most of the people in his business world did not have the slightest sus-
picion that, in his spare time, Ives was a composer—let

alone a composer of some of the most original music then yet conceived.

But there existed another Charles Ives. And what a different person this was from the insurance salesman! This second Charles Ives was known only to a few scattered friends, to his wife, and to their adopted daughter. This was the man who spent his time on a farm atop a hill in West Redding, Connecticut, wearing rough clothes, a battered hat, and the cumbersome shoes of a peasant; who led a life of almost total seclusion. He never went to parties, never attended social functions, never entertained dinner guests at home, never even went to concerts. When his day's work in insurance was completed, Ives spent his evenings—sometimes late into the night—composing. Sundays and holidays brought him no surcease from his creative preoccupation. His most intimate friends respected his basic need to be left alone, even while possibly shrugging their shoulders in amazement at a man who had no interest other than to scratch notes on paper. Fortunately, Ives had a wife who understood him, who had supreme confidence in his genius. She never complained at their lack of social diversions and seemed quite content to share his world of isolation. She never raised a skeptical eyebrow at the peculiar sounds he called music. "Mrs. Ives," he once confessed, "never once said or suggested or looked or thought that there must be something wrong with me. She never said, 'Now why don't you be good and write something nice, the way they like it?' Never. She urged me on my way to be myself and gave me her confidence."

He would write his strange compositions and then put them away in a closet and forget all about them. He never made the slightest effort to get any of his works performed, and he never submitted a single composition to a publisher. There may have been a thoroughly sound, practical reason why he preferred to keep his music to himself, to stay out of the musical marketplace. This way he could maintain his creative individuality and originality without discouragement and the severe criticism of practical musicians who would have told him that music like this would never get performed—that, indeed, it was a crazy man's music. Ives was convinced that even sophisticated musicians would not have the slightest notion of what he was trying to do.

And so, his manuscripts kept piling upon shelves in closets and in bureau drawers. He kept on writing, fully satisfied just to get his music down on paper. The only two works he had published were done at his own expense, and merely for distribution among his closest friends; they were never sent out to critics or professional musicians. One was the *Concord Sonata,* for piano, published in 1919, (together with an extended dissertation explaining his aims in writing this music, a dissertation entitled *Essays Before a Sonata,* which in recent years has been published independently of the music for general distribution). The other publication, in 1922, was *114 Songs.* This was an anthology of all the songs he had written between 1888 ("Slow March") and 1921 ("Majority"), but presented in reverse chronological order so that his last song was the first number in the anthology and his first song was the last. This publication was also preceded by a preface describing his musical goals in a totally unorthodox, and frequently amusing, manner. "This volume," he said, "is now thrown, so to speak, at the music fraternity, who for this reason will feel free to dodge it on its way—perhaps to the waste basket." Most of the songs were in a thoroughly unconventional idiom. "A song," Ives explained, "has a few rights, the same as other ordinary citizens. . . . If it happens to feel like trying to fly where humans cannot fly—to sing what cannot be sung—to walk in a cave on all fours—to tighten up its girth in blind hope and faith and try to scale mountains that are not—who shall stop it?"

In evolving his kind of unprecedented music, Ives was not just putting to practice some preconceived theory he had concocted. He was creating sounds that thundered in his head; he developed a style and structure that came to him instinctively. His very first song "Majority," was a product of his fourteenth year. In the piano accompaniment he used jarring harmonies built on intervals of seconds (the consecutive two notes of the chromatic scale). Composers had avoided harmony like this because it was so unpleasant to listen to, but Ives found such discords invigorating and fresh, and so he used them. More than twenty years later, another American composer, Henry Cowell (1897–1965), wrote many piano compositions using similar harmonies to which he gave the name of "tone clusters." Cowell, then a young man, achieved a good deal of notoriety and publicity for this practice, both in America and Europe. Ives did not dub his harmonies based on intervals of seconds "tone clusters" but he certainly anticipated Cowell in this harmonic language. Ives continued to use "tone clusters" in a good many of his later compositions —and with extraordinary effect.

This is possibly the most amazing thing about Ives' music: Many of the most advanced modern techniques and idioms which later became identified with other composers were used by him years and years before those composers thought of using them (and those composers knew nothing about Ives). Stravinsky and Milhaud, for example, shocked audiences and critics when they began using two or more different keys simultaneously (polytonality). Ives used this method again and again in his major works. In the same way Ives preceded by many years those composers who later became famous for piling one rhythm on another until a kind of primitive force is generated (polyrhythms), or for using rapidly changing meters (polymeters), or experimenting with intervals smaller than the traditional half tone of the chromatic or diatonic scales (microtonal music). After World War II, composers began experimenting with "chance music"; Ives toyed with the idea almost half a century earlier.

What Ives was aiming at—more instinctively than consciously—was to emancipate music once and for all from stultifying traditions and schoolbook rules. He wanted nothing to stand in the way of a composer's imagination. Music, he felt, must be as free as a bird to soar where it wills, not where manmade laws directed. A composer, he insisted, must be allowed to do anything his artistic conscience demanded—however unconventional or even absurd might seem what he is doing. And this is the reason why in any book on our present-day avant-garde movement, Charles Ives must be the first composer to come under discussion.

Absurdity was part of Ives' invention. In a bassoon passage in one of his orchestral works he wrote above several empty measures: "From here on, the bassoon may play anything at all." In the opening movement of a piano sonata he refused to designate a specific tempo, allowing the performer to make his own choice. Ives argued that tempo varies with what kind of a day it is when the music is being played, and what the virtuoso's feelings are when he is playing. In a violin and piano sonata he suddenly introduces a brief trumpet solo and then forgets all about that trumpet for the rest of the work. In a piano sonata he did the same thing with a flute. In one of his songs for voice and piano, a violin obbligato enters and departs without warning.

Ives could do whatever he wished because he had no ambition to write "beautiful" music, in the Classic and Romantic concept of "beautiful" music. Music to Ives was not the aural equivalent of a piece of candy delighting the palate. It was human experience—and human experience cannot be sugar-coated. It was artistic truth that Ives was seeking, or, to use his own phrase, "the inner invisible activity of truth." To express that truth he used every means he could, however much it departed from accepted practices.

Not all human experience, of course, is a bitter diet. From time to time, Ives could also be humorous or whimsical in his music. In one of his string quartets he calls the second violin "Rollo" (the only instrument to be given a name). During a long pause in one of the sections for the second violin he scribbled over empty measures: "Too hard to play, so it just can't be good music, Rollo." In *114 Songs* he added a comment that one of those songs had been written "to clear up the long disputed point, namely, which is worse, the music or the words." He sometimes indulged in parody, as in one of his symphonies where (with tongue square in cheek) he introduced a travesty on the kind of choir and organ music he had heard in church when he was a boy. He ends another symphony with a chord that includes all the notes of the chromatic scale, except one, evoking a mood of mockery. In his last two symphonies he purposely disfigures and distorts thrice-familiar American popular tunes; here, once again, the whimsical composer is indulging in a few chuckles.

A celebrated anecdote about General Ulysses S. Grant concerns a band concert attended by both General Grant and President Lincoln. When President Lincoln asked Grant if he liked the composition just performed, the General replied: "I don't know, Mr. President. You see, I know only two tunes. One of them is 'Yankee Doodle.' The other isn't."

The reason this amusing item is relevant in a chapter on Ives is because the conductor of that band concert was George Ives, the father of the composer. If Charles became such a musical iconoclast, much of the credit belongs to his father. George Ives was an extraordinary musical innovator in his own right. He was the bandmaster of the First Connecticut Heavy Artillery in General Grant's army—but his musical curiosity and interest extended far beyond the regulated repertory of army-band music. For father Ives had preceded his son in making tentative efforts at writing music with intervals smaller than the half tone, in trying to arrive at novel effects by playing two different melodies in two different keys simultaneously. Father Ives also made acoustical tests by dividing his band into several groups, placing each one in a different place in a public square and then studying the impact made by the composition when it was heard coming from several different directions. Many years later we would dub this method "directional music."

His son, Charles, was born in Danbury, Connecticut, on October 20, 1874. Charles's first teacher was his father

who taught him theory, composition, sight-reading, orchestration, piano, cornet, and the organ. The boy was well
grounded in the literature of Bach and Beethoven, but
was also taught popular songs, including those of Stephen
Foster. What the father insisted upon most in training his
son was to have him accept untraditional sounds. "You
must learn to stretch your ears!" his father would advise
him continually. He had Charles play "Swanee River" in
one key while he, the father, played the accompaniment in
an alien key. Or his father would insist that Charles play
two different melodies in two different keys at the piano
at the same time.

Charles was outstandingly musical. It was not long before
he was making music professionally. At thirteen he became
an organist at the Danbury Congregational Church. Soon
after this, he played the drums in his father's band. He
was also composing. His first piece was *Holiday Quick Step,*
a march, where he still stuck to the rule book. His father
played this piece at one of his band concerts. It is
thoroughly typical of the modesty and reticence of Charles
Ives the man that Charles Ives the boy should not only
refuse to play the drums when his composition was played
but would not even come to the concert to hear it performed!

In fact, he was just a little ashamed of his total involve-
ment in music. He later confessed: "When other boys on
Monday mornings on vacation were out driving the grocery
cart, riding horses, or playing ball, I felt all wrong to stay
in and play the piano." He himself liked both baseball and
football considerably, as a spectator and as a performer. But
he liked music more, and whenever he had to make a choice

between the ball park and the piano he made straight for the piano.

Probably because his father was a band leader, the boy Charles loved band music most of all. Whenever a band marched through the streets of Danbury (in those days it was a frequent event), Charles would follow it, listening spellbound to the music-making. Then if another band happened to come along from another direction, he would change his course to follow that group. It was at this time that he first revealed his unusual fascination for unorthodox combinations of sounds. Sometimes two bands would arrive simultaneously from opposite directions, each playing a different tune. Ives experienced a genuine thrill when the mingling of the two different melodies created a discord and joined together alien tonalities and rhythms. This experience had a permanent impact on his creativty. In some of his later orchestral works he simulated the sounds coming from two different bands approaching each other playing different selections.

Charles Ives' musical education took place at the elementary schools and the high school in Danbury, at the Hopkins Preparatory School in New Haven and, beginning with 1894, at Yale. Before he entered Yale, Ives studied the organ with a fine Danbury musician, Harry Rowe Shelley. Ives had also written, in 1888, his first unconventional piece of music, the song "Slow March" with its accompanying tone clusters (the first time such a harmonic scheme was used). While at Yale, Ives was a pupil of Horatio Parker and Dudley Buck; he played the organ at the Center Church; he wrote composition after composition, including his first symphony. Walter Damrosch, the distinguished conductor of the New York Symphony Society, tried out a part of that symphony with his orchestra early in the twentieth century and was so thoroughly confused by the changing meters, the strange combinations of tonalities, and the discords that he threw up his arms in total surrender. Damrosch never performed the symphony publicly.

What Ives was being taught in the classroom appeared, apparently, to have no effect on the kind of music he insisted on putting down on paper. As he later said: "I could not go on using the familiar chords only. I heard something else."

After being graduated from Yale in 1898 with a degree of Bachelor of Arts, Ives moved to New York where he shared an apartment with friends. His father had now been dead for some years and Ives had to find ways of supporting himself while conceiving the strange, new music which he knew would inspire only contempt from performers, publishers, and audiences, but which he had to keep on writing nevertheless. He worked as a clerk at the Mutual Life Insurance Company for a salary of $5.00 a week, but earned some extra money playing the organ at the Central Presbyterian Church.

"I heard something else," Ives once remarked. It was definitely "something else" that emerged from two compositions completed in 1901. *Steeples and Mountains* (scored for two sets of chimes and church bells, accompanied by four trumpets and four trombones, each quartet playing in unison), had each chime or bell sounding its tones in different keys. The overall effect was to produce a complex mass of sounds in a polytonal style. So advanced of its time was this music, in fact so without precedent, that it had to wait sixty-four years to get performed—on July 30,

1965, with Lukas Foss directing the New York Philharmonic Orchestra.

More significant still was the Second Symphony, the second major work to come in 1901. This work owes its importance not only to the advanced methods and unusual sounds we encounter there, but also because this was thoroughly *American* music at a time when most American composers were merely echoing European voices. Ives himself explained that this symphony "expresses the musical feelings of the Connecticut country around here (Redding and Danbury, Connecticut) in the 1890s, the music of the country folk. It is full of the tunes they sang and played then." This is the first of Ives' works in which he indulged in what later became a practice of quoting popular American tunes. In the first movement we catch a brief quotation from "Columbia, the Gem of the Ocean" (heard not as a basic theme but as a hurriedly stated countersubject in the horns to a rugged principal theme of his own invention). In the third movement, American church music of the 1860s, 1870s, and 1880s is parodied. The fourth movement is a patchwork of tunes by Stephen Foster, including "De Camptown Races" and "Old Black Joe," with all kinds of country dances and barn melodies gliding over or comingling with them. This, the finale of the symphony, comes to its culmination with a repetition of "Columbia, the Gem of the Ocean."

This symphony is typical Ives in that it combines the sacred and the profane, the popular and the serious; also in that Ives gives in to his weakness for whimsy by combining popular tunes contrapuntally (and discordantly) with themes by Johann Sebastian Bach, and with short quotations from the works of Wagner, Bruckner, Brahms, and

Dvořák. But as Leonard Bernstein put it so well in his program notes for the New York Philharmonic Orchestra when he performed this symphony: "Ives' symphony never *sounds* like Brahms and Wagner and the rest—it sounds like Ives. . . . The European spirit has been Americanized, just as a Bach chorale gets Americanized into a Methodist hymn; it achieves a new tonal quality. Ives goes even further by tossing bits of Americana into this European soup-pot, thus making a new brew out of it, very American in flavor."

It took fifty years for the Second Symphony to get performed in its entirety for the first time, when Bernstein conducted it with the New York Philharmonic on February 22, 1951. Bernstein invited Ives to the première but Ives turned it down in no uncertain terms. Bernstein then offered Ives privacy by allowing him to listen to a special performance of the symphony with nobody else in the auditorium. Once again Ives said he was not interested. But when Bernstein conducted the symphony on a Sunday afternoon concert that was being broadcast nationally, Ives sneaked downstairs into the kitchen where his cook kept her radio (the only radio in the house) to listen to his work —his first *hearing* of what he had heard in his mind's ear so long ago. When the performance ended he was so delighted he came out of the kitchen and did a jig.

Following the writing of his Second Symphony, Ives continually sought his inspiration, stimulation, and subject matter from American scenes, backgrounds, customs, history, holidays. In doing so he was not pursuing a nationalistic course, as he confessed; nationalism, he said, was pursuing *him*. Ives felt that a *real* American composer must perforce write *American* music since as a human being he is the sum total of his American orientations and experiences. Any American composer who imitated Brahms, Wagner, or Debussy, or any other of the famous European composers, was just a compiler of thematic material, Ives said, and not a genuine creative force. To Ives, *American* music came as naturally, as instinctively, as inevitably as did the use of his quixotic methods and iconoclastic techniques. His through-and-through Americanism as composer was perhaps almost as important a contribution to music as was his modernistic style.

In his now quite familiar Third Symphony, written between 1901 and 1904, Ives carried over into his music the spirit and some of the tunes of American camp meetings popular in nineteenth-century Connecticut. Sometimes in this symphony Ives quoted such old American hymns as "O for a Thousand Tongues" and "Just as I Am." In the middle movement, Ives describes the games children played at camp meetings while their parents prayed. "This music," said Lawrence Gilman, a distinguished music critic in New York, and one of the first to recognize Ives' true importance, "is as indubitably American in impulse and spiritual texture as the prose of Jonathan Edwards." (Jonathan Edwards, the famous eighteenth-century American theologian and philosopher, was the author of the first American book to gain the respect and interest of Europe, published in 1754.)

After working as an insurance clerk, Ives formed his own company in 1906 which, three years later, became the firm of Ives and Myrick. This agency developed in time into a highly influential and prosperous business. Meanwhile, on June 8, 1908, he married Harmony Twichell. She was the daughter of a clergyman in Hartford, Connecticut—a beautiful young lady who had been trained to be a nurse. The Twichells were good friends of Mark Twain. One day, Harmony brought Charles to visit Mark Twain. Feeling incumbent upon himself to pass judgment on the man who was trying to win Harmony as a wife, Twain examined Ives from top to bottom. "Well," commented the author at last, "the fore seems all right. Turn him around and let's see the aft." Ives, who enjoyed a quip as well as the next man, took such delight in this remark that he kept quoting it throughout his life.

The Iveses first made their home in a modest New York apartment. They never had children of their own but raised an adopted daughter, Edith. The ensuing years saw Ives doggedly pursuing two divurgent paths. One was his business, which made him prosperous, and enabled him to buy a house in New York and a farm in West Redding, Connecticut; the other was his music, to which he devoted himself every spare minute he could find.

In 1903, Ives began working on *Three Places in New England* for chamber orchestra. It took him eight years to finish it. Here his inspiration was New England geography and history. The first movement gives a picture of Saint-Gaudens in Boston Common (as the title of the movement indicates); but the second section, "Colonel Shaw and his Colored Regiment," recalls the era of Stephen Foster and the period of the Civil War. In the second movement ("Putnam's Camp, Redding, Connecticut") Ives describes a small park where General Putnam's forces made their camp in 1778–1779. Here Ives evokes a fourth of July picnic in this park. Reminiscences of the Revolutionary War that this historic place brings to the mind of a child, and the games children played there, are elaborated upon. Revolutionary War songs and marches are quoted; a violent discord is achieved when two marches, in two different keys and in different rhythms, are played simultaneously by two bands. The third movement, "The Housatonic at Stockbridge," is a tonal scenic painting, but even here Ives does not avoid strange new sounds. At one point a solo violin plays in a rhythm totally different from that in the rest of the orchestra. Through the complex texture of other sections atonal and polytonal passages continually pierce.

While working on *Three Places in New England,* Ives completed his most important work for the piano—the now famous *Concord Sonata* upon which he labored between 1909 and 1915. This music re-creates, as Ives himself has explained, "the spirit of the literature, the philosophy, and the men of Concord, Massachusetts, of over half a century." The first movement is an interpretation of the prose and poetry of Ralph Waldo Emerson. It is here that Ives refused to designate a specific tempo marking, leaving the tempo entirely to the discretion and will of the performer. "The same essay or poem of Emerson," Ives explained, "may bring a slightly different feeling when read at sunrise or when read at sunset." Music inspired by such an essay or poem, said Ives, must be allowed similar latitude. Another famous American author, Nathaniel Hawthorne, is the subject of the second movement where Ives, in one section, instructs the performer to use a ruler or a strip of wood to cover a two-octave tone cluster. The third movement is entitled "The Alcotts." Amos Bronson Alcott had been a distinguished philosopher and educator, and the father of Louisa May Alcott, the author of such ever-popular books for the young as *Little Women* and *Little*

Men. Since the Alcott children were always practicing Beethoven's music on the piano, Ives interpolated into this movement the first four notes of Beethoven's Fifth Symphony. The sonata ends with "Thoreau," a musical tribute to the eminent author of *Walden*. This is an idyllic piece of music (when compared to some of the primitive and wild outbursts of sound that preceded it). A short flute solo enters suddenly to enhance the serenity, because, Ives explained, Thoreau liked to hear flute music at dusk at Walden.

The year 1916 saw the completion of another Ives master work, his monumental Fourth Symphony. This is a hybrid work in that the first three movements consist of orchestral transcriptions of earlier Ives nonsymphonic works. In the first movement Ives poses the question of the "what" and the "why" asked of life by the spirit of man. The rest of the symphony is intended to answer the question.

In the first movement, three hymns are quoted: "The Sweet Bye-and-Bye," "Nearer, my God, to Thee," and a choral episode with which the movement ends, "Watchman, Tell Us of the Night." The second movement, which opens with a noisy and distorted suggestion of "Marching Through Georgia," was suggested by the "Hawthorne" movement of the *Concord Sonata*. Various popular American tunes—each appearing to pursue its individual course without any apparent recognition of the other tunes—weave and interweave in this complicated tonal texture: "Yankee Doodle," "Turkey in the Straw," "Columbia, the Gem of the Ocean." The third movement is an orchestral transcription of a movement from Ives' String Quartet No. 1. In structure it is a double fugue with two hymns providing the thematic subjects: "From Greenland's Icy Mountains" and "All Hail Power."

Ives never did get around to completing the finale of his symphony. But he did leave behind a mass of disorganized manuscripts comprising random musical thoughts, various sequences, innumerable odds and ends which he had scribbled into various notebooks and on pieces of papers and stuffed into desk drawers, in an old trunk, and on closet shelves. After Ives' death, several scholars spent a number of years not only to piece together all these disconnected items into a coherent unity but even to decipher Ives' jumbled notation. The scholars did their job so well that their final product became authenic Ives—indeed, the crown of the entire symphony. One of the principal ideas in this finale is "Memorial Slow March" which Ives had once written for organ and which had been derived from the hymn, "Nearer, my God, to Thee." Other popular American melodies are also introduced ("Marching Through Georgia," "Turkey in the Straw," "De Camptown Races," "Yankee Doodle," "Columbia, the Gem of the Ocean"). These are presented in fleeting fragments that are as distorted as figures seen through a broken or misshapen mirror, and sometimes juxtaposed polytonally with Ives' own episodic ideas. What ensues is a kind of tonal explosion, sending splinters of themes flying pell mell into the air in all directions. Yet there is no feeling of confusion or chaos. What Leonard Bernstein said of the Second Symphony holds true for the Fourth Symphony as well: "Instead of making a hodgepodge, [the movement] turns out to make a real work, original, eccentric, naïve, and full of charm as a New England village green. On top of all this, there is always that fresh, awkward, endearing, primitive style of his, where all the rules got broken: gauche endings, unfinished phrases, wrong voice-leadings, and inexplicable orchestration. . . . That's what so touching about all this use of Americana; it comes to us full of Ives' brave resolve to be American, to write American music in the face of a diffident and uninterested public." Indeed, to the distinguished music critic, Alfred Frankenstein, "the idea of the finale as a triumphant summation and spiritual affirmation here meets its most profound and significant challenge. In many ways, this may well be the most original and important movement in any of the symphonies by America's greatest composer."

It takes an immense orchestra to perform this work, supplemented by a brass band, a greatly expanded percussion section, and a chorus. So vast are the forces and so complicated is the musical texture that three conductors are needed for the performance. ("There is one section where twenty-seven different rhythms are played simultaneously.) Leopold Stokowski, who (with the assistance of two young conductors) led the symphony's world première in New York on April 26, 1965, regards it as one of the most difficult pieces of music he had ever worked with during his long career spanning half a century. So much preparation was required before the performance that a special grant of $8,000 was given by the Rockefeller Foundation to defray the expense of the many additional rehearsals required to whip the work into shape, as the three conductors worked painstakingly phrase by phrase, sometimes measure by measure, to fit all the disparate parts of this giant musical jigsaw puzzle into a complete tonal picture.

By 1918, Ives had written his most important works. After that he produced his music by dribs and drabs until

1928 when he gave up composition for good. As he was a victim of diabetes and a disturbed nervous system, his hands trembled so by 1928 that he was incapable of doing any writing. Besides he had by now become fully convinced he had exhausted himself creatively. What he had to say, he had said; what he had hoped to accomplish in changing the character and language of music he had accomplished. And he was not the kind of man who would permit himself the luxury of repeating himself.

His health deteriorated quickly from this point on. A heart attack depleted his energies and physical resources. He suffered from cataracts of both eyes. Broken in health, he gave up all his business activities in 1930 and went into total retirement on his farm in West Redding, withdrawing completely from the world, aloof even from his close friends, whose visits became increasingly rare. He never read newspapers. He refused to allow either a radio or phonograph within his own living quarters until the last two years of his life (the only radio in the house up to then was the one belonging to his cook). His main diversions were to play the piano as best he could with his quivering, weakened fingers (always Ives' own music), and to take long solitary walks absorbed in contemplation. He had no interest in what was happening in the music world where composers now became famous for methods he himself had devised many years earlier. He maintained a total indifference to recognition of any kind. He did not want his music to get played.

But in spite of the fact he never contacted a performer or publisher, his works—slowly but inevitably—were beginning to receive a public hearing. One of the first of his significant works to be performed was a movement from his

Fourth Symphony, on January 29, 1927, in New York. In 1931, Nicolas Slonimsky conducted, also in New York, the world première of *Three Places in New England.*

In spite of his every effort to preserve his privacy and obscurity, Ives was beginning to attract increasing attention. On January 30, 1938, John Kirkpatrick gave the world première of the *Concord Sonata.* At that time Lawrence Gilman, in his review, called it "the greatest music composed by an American in impulse and implication." In 1941, Aaron Copland devoted a chapter in praise of Ives' *114 Songs* in his book, *Our American Music.* Fame for Ives was now only a few years off. On April 5, 1946, Ives' Third Symphony was heard for the first time—forty years after it had been written. Suddenly the world of music sat up and took notice of its composer. The New York Music Critics' Circle gave it a special commendation, but more significant still was the fact that the symphony received the Pulitzer Prize in music. When informed about the latter honor, Ives' reaction was one of anger rather than exhilaration. "Prizes," he exclaimed, "are badges of mediocrity. Prizes are for boys. I'm grown up."

Winning the Pulitzer Prize robbed Ives of the seclusion from public attention he had guarded jealously for many years. That its recipient was a total recluse devoid of any vanity; that he was in total contempt of public attention and adulation; that he created music almost half a century ahead of its time—all this was choice material for feature stories in the newspapers and magazines. Letters of praise or inquiries about himself, his hobbies and opinions, or requests for his photograph poured into his farm. Candidates for doctorates in music sent in for analyses of his works. A European phrenologist wanted an opportunity to study his head. A psychologist asked for a chance to give him a Rorschach test. Music libraries pleaded for some of his manuscripts. Writers asked for personal interviews.

In fame, as in neglect, Ives remained himself, He answered nobody. He refused to see anybody. Under no circumstance would he allow himself to be photographed. (Only one photograph of his adult years exists—an old and indistinct one made many years ago.) It was impossible to entice him to attend a performance of any of his music. He made it perfectly clear that now more than ever was he eager to be left alone. But the more he avoided attention the more he attracted it. His biography, written by Henry and Sidney Cowell, was published in 1955. Performers everywhere seemed to compete with one another for the honor of introducing one of his yet many unperformed compositions.

Only one music critic managed, through the intervention of Mrs. Ives, to invade the seemingly impenetrable fortress of Ives' privacy. He was Howard Taubman, the music critic of *The New York Times*. Mrs. Ives welcomed him on the porch and asked him to wait until her husband gave the signal he was ready to be seen. Suddenly Taubman heard the pounding of a cane on the floor from inside the house. This was Ives' way of informing his wife that Taubman could now enter. "Charles E. Ives was standing in a large room. . . . At first glance he looked like a Yankee patriarch. . . . He was gaunt and wiry, and with the help of his cane he stood up straight so that there was only the faintest suggestion of stooping shoulders. The gray, scraggly beard gave his lean face an appearance of roundness. . . . He wore rough country clothes—sturdy shoes, blue denim trousers, a faded blue shirt without a tie, an old darned sweater, and gray tweed jacket. He took off his dark glasses and looked at you, and the eyes were bright and alert."

This is apparently the only interview Ives ever gave. Though he was reticent about talking about his work, he did concede that he had anticipated most of the innovations other composers had since made famous. This fact did not bother him at all. "That's not my fault," he remarked quietly and stoically.

By the time Ives died in New York on May 19, 1954, (following an unsuccessful operation), there were few to deny him a place of first importance among American composers; few to fail to remark that he was the first composer to create authentically American music; few to neglect to note that he was the first of the great musical adventurers of the twentieth century, possibly one of the greatest. Today the music of Charles Ives is in the basic repertory. Virtually everything important has been recorded—including a handsome album comprising all four symphonies.

The limelight Ives had so scrupulously avoided all his life now glows on him and his music with a blazing incandescence.

II | *He developed a new musical system.*

Arnold Schoenberg

(1874–1951)

When I first met Arnold Schoenberg in Vienna, in 1930, I was (to say the least) taken aback at the sight of the man who stood before me. He was small, slight, with sunken cheeks, a man obviously victimized by asthma. He seemed so frail that I felt a puff of a breeze could destroy him. Yet this fragile body was the receptacle of a will so indomitable and so inflexible, of a courage and a spirit so unconquerable, that for years he had been able to stand virtually alone against the entire music world, to receive without surcease some of the most vicious and most venemous attacks any composer has known, Wagner not excluded. These attacks and abuses came not only from those diehard reactionaries who cling to the past and are in horror of the progress of the future, but even from many progressive-minded, world-famous musicians. (What was it that Richard Strauss told me in 1930 when I informed him I was going to visit Schoenberg in Vienna? "Anybody can be a composer who is not interested in producing *music.*") Schoenberg had accepted blow after blow that would have felled an ox, and yet he remained standing proud and erect, convinced of the truth of his musical gospel, never for one moment doubting that the future belonged to him. Oh, yes, there was a small band of dedicated pupils and disciples who not only believed in him completely and unquestioningly but who also had adopted *his* way of writing music—Alban Berg, for example, and Anton Webern. But these men, all of whom regarded Schoenberg not only as their teacher but also as a prophet in music, were for many years people without reputations, influence, or money. Besides, on the rare occasions when *their* works were played, they, too, were maliciously maligned. Their adoration notwithstanding, then, Schoenberg was very much alone. The rest of the music world was lined up solidly against him. And yet in time Schoenberg would be the composer responsible for one of the most influential and revolutionary changes in the techniques of music that history has known.

For Schoenberg was the one who developed a new musical doctrine that broke completely with the past, a doctrine popularly known as the twelve-tone system or the twelve-tone technique, and sometimes as dodecaphony. The older methods, the older idioms, the older points of view, the older aesthetics of music—all of which had served the past musicmasters so well for three centuries—were obsolete. So said Schoenberg. *His* concept of music—how it should sound, how it should be constructed—was a truth that would in time (he felt) so thoroughly replace the old truths that all composers would be compelled to use his method, a method in which dissonance replaced consonance.

And so this little man absorbed the mental and spiritual

punishment that seems to be the fate of every prophet unfortunate enough to anticipate the future. He did so, however, not without mental anguish, by any means, nor without towering rage. As Cassandra, to whom Apollo gave the most tortured punishment of all, he knew what lay in store in the future, but nobody believed what he was prophesying. Schoenberg is perhaps the musical personification of this Greek character. It is impossible to describe adequately the inner torment suffered by this composer as year after year he saw his music rejected and despised, inspire riots in concert halls, arouse the most poisonous vituperation from critics. But to stoop to conquer, to turn back the hands of time—this Schoenberg refused to do. And so he continued going his own lonely way without a faltering step and without digression. You had only to look into his fierce blazing eyes to realize that for him there was no such thing as compromise. And he lived long enough to see himself and his theories completely vindicated.

Listen to what some of the cognoscenti of the 1910s and 1920s had to say about him. "Schoenberg's tone poem is not just filled with wrong notes. It is a fifty-minute long protracted wrong note. One deals here with a man either devoid of all sense or who takes his listeners for fools." Thus spake Ludwig Karpath, the German critic. At the première of Schoenberg's *Chamber Symphony*, in 1907, a riot erupted in the hall. Sounds of disapproval from the audience became deafening. Police were called in when people began exchanging blows. One lady in that audience went to court to sue Schoenberg for damages, insisting that she had become chronically psychoneurotic from listening to his music; and one of her witnesses was a psychiatrist who testified that it *was* possible to develop mental illness from

Schoenberg's kind of music. In 1912 another highly regarded German critic, Otto Taubman, said of Schoenberg's
Pierrot Lunaire: "If this is music, then I pray my Creator
not to let me hear music again." In that same year an English
critic wrote of Schoenberg's *Five Pieces for Orchestra* that
it "resembled the wailings of a tortured soul and suggested
nothing so much as the disordered fancies of delirium or
the fearsome, imaginary terrors of a highly nervous infant."

These and similar critical missiles attacked Schoenberg
with deadly accuracy each time a new work of his was given.
Even an audience as staid and dignified as the one in Philadelphia could vent its fury, with shouts and hisses, when
Leopold Stokowski conducted the Philadelphia Orchestra
in Schoenberg's *Orchestral Variations* in the 1920s.

And the little man took all this abuse without for one
moment doubting himself or his music. He heard Stravinsky speak of him as "Little Herr Modernsky" and he saw
Stravinsky brush aside all of Schoenberg's works with a con-
temptuous sweep of the hand as if it were just so much rub-
bish. As late as 1944, when many critics and musicians were
acknowledging that Schoenberg's place with the masters of
twentieth-century music could no longer be disputed, Schoenberg was denied a Guggenheim Fellowship (which paid
$2,500 for a year), apparently being deemed unworthy of
the grant in comparison to those who competed with him!
At that time, Schoenberg's basic income was the $38-a-
month pension from the University of California in Los
Angeles, and he needed the Fellowship to support his family while he completed his monumental opera *Moses and
Aaron.* Schoenberg—thanks to the "far-sighted" wisdom of
his judges, not one of whom was worthy of shining his

shoes—did not get that Fellowship, and *Moses and Aaron* remains today without a third act.

What was Schoenberg's reaction to all the humiliation heaped upon him through the years? As far back as 1912 he said: "The second half of the century will compensate by excessive praise for the lack of understanding that my work received in the first half of the century." In saying this he was once again prophetic. In the second half of the present century, Stravinsky, now an old man, completely rejected the neoclassic style he had been favoring for more than a quarter of a century to embrace dodecaphony exclusively. Now—with Schoenberg dead—Stravinsky could say (when informed that Schoenberg had once been rejected for the Guggenheim Fellowship): "Four more measures of *Moses and Aaron* would have been a greater contribution to music than all the works produced by all the recipients of the Guggenheim Fellowship." And the University that could afford only $38 a month to Schoenberg is today proud of an Arnold Schoenberg Building for its music department that probably cost several hundred thousand dollars to build.

Stravinsky was not the only convert to the Schoenberg musical religion; not by any means. Major composers all over the civilized world—indeed, some of the most important composers the post World War II period has produced —have made Schoenberg's technique the basis for their own creation. Aaron Copland, late in his career, found the twelve-tone technique valuable for some of his compositions, and Leonard Bernstein has used it in parts of his two symphonies, *The Age of Anxiety* and *Kaddish*. Here is a partial list of some of the other distinguished composers to adopt dodecaphony: Tadeux Baird and Witold Lutoslawski in Poland; Robert Gebhard and Humphrey Searle in England; Bo Nillson and Karl-Birger Blomdahl in Sweden; Rolf Liebermann in Switzerland; Pierre Boulez in France; Hans Werner Henze and Karlheinz Stockhausen in Germany; Luigi Dallapiccola, Luigi Nono, and Luciano Berio in Italy; Alberto Ginastera in Buenos Aires; and in the United States, Roger Sessions, Wallingford Riegger, Leon Kirchner, Ernest Krenek, among others. Operas now recognized by acknowledged authorities as among the most vital and compelling musical theater of our century are in the twelve-tone technique. Among them are Berg's *Lulu,* Dallapiccola's *The Prisoner (Il prigioniero),* Henze's *The Stag King (König Hirsch),* Schoenberg's *Moses and Aaron,* and Roger Sessions' *Montezuma.* Here is the opinion of Nicolas Slonimsky, the noted musicologist: "No living composer has escaped Schoenberg's attraction. His system of twelve-tone writing is now universally acknowledged as the most potent musical doctrine of the century." One might go even one step further than Slonimsky by suggesting that Schoenberg's musical doctrine has exerted possibly the greatest influence of any system in music history since when, centuries ago, the church modes were discarded in favor of the major and minor scales, or since the time when homophony replaced polyphony.

In order to understand and appreciate what Schoenberg has accomplished, and the forces that led him to accomplish it, let us follow this genius on his lonely journey from its very beginnings.

Arnold Schoenberg was the son of middle-class Jewish parents, born in Vienna on September 13, 1874. Early in life, the boy Schoenberg was converted to Catholicism, but he never strictly followed any religious ritual. His sole religion was music, though it was some years before he proved that he possessed any talent for the art. He began studying the violin when he was eight, and produced his first compositions four years later. All the while he was attending elementary school for his academic education.

When Arnold was sixteen his father died. This made it necessary for the boy to start earning his living. He left school to become a bank clerk. Music was not abandoned. Without the help of a teacher he learned to play the cello well enough to collaborate in performances of chamber music. He was also doing a good deal of composing. One of his pieces attracted the interest of an influential Viennese musician, Alexander von Zemlinsky, who accepted Schoenberg as a pupil in theory. This was the only time when Schoenberg received any formal musical instruction. Zemlinsky welcomed Schoenberg into his household more as an adopted son than as pupil or protégé. As cellist, Schoenberg joined an orchestra then conducted by Zemlinsky, and in 1895 he found a job leading an amateur chorus. Through Zemlinsky, Schoenberg became friendly with a group of young, progressive-minded musicians whose discussions, arguments, hates, and enthusiasms he absorbed hungrily, an experience which helped to develop him into a knowledgeable musician.

These young musicians, and Schoenberg with them, used to gather at the Landtmann Café next to the Burgtheater (the café is still there today). Over coffee, generously topped with whipped cream (a Viennese delicacy), they would speak rapturously about their musical god—Richard Wagner. Wagner represented to these young men "the art of the future." It was not long before Schoenberg joined his young friends in falling completely under the spell of that great master of the music drama. Up to now in his compositions Schoenberg's model for emulation had been Brahms. As a follower of Brahms, Schoenberg had written the String Quartet in D major in 1897 (introduced in Vienna a year later), and several songs which were also written in 1897 but which did not get heard until 1900. Now, just as a new century was at hand, Schoenberg started abandoning his complete dedication to Brahms, to Brahms' concentration on absolute as opposed to programmatic music, and to Brahms' personal creative mannerisms. Schoenberg now adopted the kind of dramatic, sensuous, chromatic style and harmonic language which identified Wagner so unmistakably.

The first of Schoenberg's works to survive—indeed one of the most frequently heard of all of Schoenberg's works to the present time—points up to the total conversion of the young composer to Wagner. This composition is *Transfigured Night (Verklärte Nacht)*, completed as a sextet in 1899, but transcribed for chamber orchestra in 1917, the version in which it is the most famous. (Subsequently Schoenberg also transcribed the composition for full symphony orchestra.) *Transfigured Night* was a tone poem based on a literary program—Richard Dehmel's poem *Woman and the World (Weib und die Welt)*. The poem describes how a man and a woman are walking in the moonlight. Slowly, hesitantly, the woman confesses to the man she will soon bear a child, but that the child's father is not the man who now is her companion. There is a good deal of emotional disturbance as the confession is told and heard. But in the end her companion finds it in his heart to understand and forgive. They fall into an embrace, then resume their moonlight walk. Redemption has come through love, which, by no coincidence at all, is a subject that had also been a particular favorite of Wagner and which dominated the texts of his operas, *The Flying Dutchman, Tannhäuser,* and *Lohengrin.*

The programmatic theme of redemption was not the only thing that was Wagnerian about *Transfigured Night.* Undeniably Wagnerian, too, is Schoenberg's music, with its surging climaxes, its rich and luscious harmonies and contrapunal textures, and its chromaticisms. Parts of the tone poem sound as if, while writing it, Schoenberg could not free his subconscious creative mind from *Tristan and Isolde.* A D minor motive for violas and cellos evokes the brooding, haunting atmosphere of a moonlit night, the atmosphere intensified with tremolos in the low register that are so typically Wagnerian. And now a violin solo rises in the upper register above the shimmering Wagnerian harmonies. It was the woman beginning her confession. A brief exchange follows between the instruments, as the woman and man converse softly. The music grows agitated, for the woman's confession is not something a man can take lightly; the voices of the chamber orchestra are spun into a web of sound in which various brief motives, like Wagnerian leading themes, grow, change, and combine into a continuous sensuous fabric.

Transfigured Night was not a success when it was heard for the first time (in Vienna on March 18, 1902), but this was mainly because six instruments were not enough to do justice to the material. Its transcription for chamber orchestra in 1917, however, made the composition famous.

Long before *Transfigured Night* became popular, Schoenberg had completed a second work over which once again there hovered the immense shadow of Wagner—this time not the Wagner of *Tristan and Isolde* but the Wagner of the *Ring of the Nibelungs*. This second Schoenberg composition was of truly Wagnerian dimensions: a setting of nineteen poems by Jens Peter Jacobsen requiring an orchestra of some one hundred and forty members, a narrator, five solo voices, three male choruses, and an eight-part mixed chorus. So vast was Schoenberg's structure that he had to have manufactured for him special note paper containing forty-eight staves, instead of the more usual dozen to twenty, in order to have room for all the instruments and voices.

This work was begun in 1899 and was basically completed in 1901 (though the final chorus and the orchestration were delayed for ten years). Called the *Songs of Gurre (Gurre-Lieder)*, it described the love of King Waldemar I of Denmark for Tove, to whom he presented the castle of Gurre as a gift. The Queen of Denmark murders Tove, an act that leads the king to reject God. The work ends dramatically with a sweeping vision of the ride of Death and a chorus singing a hymn to the rising sun.

One of the most poignant sections in this giant work is "The Song of the Wood Dove," where the dove sings to his forest friends a lament for the death of Tove. If there is any doubt of the way Wagner had infected Schoenberg this section alone would dispel it forcefully. We could almost place it somewhere within the context of the *Ring of the Nibelungs* and pass it off as one of the famous Wagnerian female narratives, say one by Waltraute, or by Erda.

The *Gurre-Lieder* received its first performance in Vienna on February 23, 1913. It scored a monumental success. The audience sprang to its feet to cheer the composer, following the resplendent hymn to the sun. Again and again the audience shouted to the composer to come to the stage and take a bow. Schoenberg stubbornly refused to leave his seat in the gallery; in fact, as soon as the acclaim burst forth, he fled from the hall. For by 1913, Schoenberg had already become a bitter man who had undergone more than one experience of having been mutilated by critics and audiences. It gave him no pleasure to see this same public so enthusiastic about music he had written many years earlier and whose style and artistic aims he had long since rejected. Explaining his refusal to come to the stage after the *Gurre-Lieder* concert he said: "For years, those people who cheered me tonight refused to recognize me. Why should I thank them for appreciating me now?"

A good deal had happened to Schoenberg the composer between 1901, when he wrote the *Gurre-Lieder,* and a dozen years later when it received its world première. His musical thinking, and his style and technique, had undergone a radical transformation. That the cheering crowds were honoring the *Gurre-Lieder* meant nothing to him, for the style he had adopted in that work was to him now "old hat." For a long time now he had been producing a *new* kind of music. Since that new music had been so decisively rejected by the music world, Schoenberg could find little comfort or pleasure in the fact that a work of his which he now regarded as outmoded was being well received.

Perhaps the most important change in Schoenberg had been his total emancipation from Wagner. With the mammoth *Gurre-Lieder* Schoenberg had exhausted his own potential for writing post-Romantic Wagnerian music— and Schoenberg knew it. He was now becoming increasingly impatient with those huge, massive works with their layers upon layers of harmony and counterpoint. To progress to even larger works with ever richer harmonic and instrumental treatment would be to produce, Schoenberg sensed, music that would collapse under the weight of its ponderosity and pretentions. In short, to put it as simply as possible, Schoenberg was thoroughly fed up with grandiloquent, grandiose, sensuous utterances which characterized Wagner and his imitators. Schoenberg now experienced an irresistible need to produce music that was, by contrast, simple, brief, precise, thoroughly objective, unemotional. He also became convinced that the old ideas about melody, harmony, tonality, and consonance had outlived their usefulness. New ones had to be evolved if music were to survive as a vital, living art.

At this critical juncture in his thinking he came into contact with the paintings of Oskar Kokoschka, a Viennese artist who was one of the earliest expressionist painters. Seeing on canvas the austerity, the bare lines, the distorted designs of Kokoschka's work—an art thoroughly divorced from the world of reality—pointed to Schoenberg a direction he now must take in his music. That direction was Expressionism.

The dozen years separating the writing and première of the *Gurre-Lieder* saw changes not only in Schoenberg's musical outlook and style but also in his personal life. At the home of his teacher, Zemlinsky, he frequently met Zemlinsky's sister, Mathilde. Schoenberg and Mathilde fell in love and were married on October 7, 1901. The necessity of supporting himself and his wife compelled him to seek a menial post in Berlin: conducting popular music in a cabaret. He was driven to do other hack work as well, such as orchestrating operettas and writing potboilers. But he was busy with serious composition at the same time, completing the *Gurre-Lieder,* and producing still another Wagnerian-type composition, the tone poem *Pelleas und Melisande* (based on the same play by Maurice Maeterlinck which Debussy had just used for his immortal impressionist opera of that name). Minor recognition as a serious composer came to Schoenberg in 1902 when he won the Franz Liszt stipend, made possible through the influence of Germany's most famous composer, Richard Strauss (also a perfect Wagnerite!). Many years later when Schoenberg abandoned Wagner for his own idiom Strauss had only contempt for his protégé.

One year of musical self-degradation was enough for Schoenberg. He returned to Vienna in 1903. Never again would he lower his standards, be it for a regular income he needed so badly, or for public approval. He worked harder than ever developing his own musical ideas and methods. Between 1904 and 1908 he completed a set of six songs; the first *Chamber Symphony (Kammersymphonie);* the String Quartet, Op. 10; pieces for the piano; and the *Five Pieces for Orchestra.* He gathered around him a small group of pupils and disciples, whose musical lifework would be deeply grounded in the soil of their teacher's idiom and aesthetics, and who looked upon him as their "master in the highest sense of the word," as Anton Webern once remarked. This group includes (besides Webern and Alban Berg, the two most famous today) Egon Wellesz, Erwin Stein, and several others.

It was after his return to Vienna in 1903, and in the compositions completed during the next five years, that Schoenberg began evolving a new language by becoming the father of musical Expressionism.

Expressionism (possibly the starting point of the twentieth-century revolution in music) is the other side of the coin of Impressionism. In the latter, the composers (masters like Debussy and Ravel) respond personally to their music, trying to capture the emotions and feelings a subject arouses in them rather than to describe that subject tonally. Expressionism on the other hand represents the total obliteration of self by the composer. Through a thoroughly objective approach the composer removes his own emotional responses from his writing, which he strips of all its trimmings and reduces down to its barest essentials.

Take, for example, the painter. Through abstraction he seeks a pure absolute form of art governed by its own laws, an art divorced from the everyday world just as it is divorced from the creator's inmost feelings. When Picasso—surely the most famous expressionist painter of our times—said "I paint what I *think* and not what I *see*," he was expressing the expressionist's credo. Thought processes, not emotional ones, are the guiding forces. The true aesthetic aim of the aesthetic painter is not to express life's experiences. "The material constituents," said Thomas Craven, the art critic, "the actual mud and oil when arrestingly consolidated, contains the true aesthetic aim."

In other words, the sensual perception is unimportant, the emotional response is unimportant, the authentic reproduction of the subject is unimportant. What *is* important is design, or what Thomas Craven called "a composition in the same sense that a pile of neatly arranged bricks is a composition." The interest in the painting lies in "the skill, the orderliness, the novelty of the arrangement," while the picture itself "represents nothing . . . even when dealing with the human form."

Similar principles began governing Schoenberg's musical writing soon after the turn of the twentieth century. He rejected Wagnerism for Expressionism. More than that he was beginning to depart permanently from those basic tenets of music-making that the world's foremost composers had been propounding for centuries.

As an expressionist composer, Schoenberg aimed to strip music of human emotion, feelings, relationships. He sought a logic of musical thought as concise as a dictionary definition, as exact as a mathematical formula. He became a musical anarchist. Away with consonance that demanded that music must sound pleasant to the ear! Schoenberg felt free to use any combinations of notes he wished, and the combinations he chose were discords. Away with a basic tonality which compelled music to stick basically and always return to a given key! Musical thought, Schoenberg insisted, should be free to move wherever it wished. It could begin in any key, progress to any key and end in any key the composer chose. And so, Schoenberg arrived at atonality. He was the first composer to make extensive use of this method that negated the tonal practices of centuries.

Away with that type of vocal melody that had to be tuneful and worked out according to rule! Schoenberg wanted the voice to have the freedom of movement to progress where it wished without restriction. And so, Schoenberg devised a technique that came to be known as "songspeech" ("*Sprechstimme*" or "*Sprechgesang*"). Here the pitch is indicated, with the voice sliding up and down to the next indicated pitch in a highly unmelodious, uneuphonious manner.

And so, long before the *Gurre-Lieder* was introduced to the world—a work in which Schoenberg was still clinging to the apron strings of Wagner—Schoenberg wrote the first piece of atonal music ever attempted. This took place in 1907 in the finale of his String Quartet, Op. 10, which calls for a soprano solo. This is the reason why some historians look upon 1907 as one of the decisive turning points in twentieth-century music. In this quartet the tonal center is completely eliminated only in the finale movement (the rest of the work being in the key of F-sharp minor). In this epoch-making composition, the soprano is heard in lines by the poet Stefan George. "With the first notes corresponding to the words 'I feel the air of other planets,' " says W. W. Cobbett, "the hearer is . . . in a new tone world."

Then, in 1908, Schoenberg produced his first work that is atonal from beginning to end, the *Three Piano Pieces,* Op. 11. Discords spill over one another. Themes are no longer melodic but fragmentary. This practice is followed even more boldly in the *Five Pieces for Orchestra,* Op. 16, in 1909. Here freedom from rule and tradition has been achieved so completely that an English critic in the *Morning Post* wrote: "Modern intellect has advanced beyond elementary noise. Schoenberg has not."

After having adopted atonality, Schoenberg invented "song-speech." This was a new kind of declamation where the rhythm is always free rather than following set patterns and which permitted the voice to swoop up and down at will to indicated pitches. This is another milestone in Schoenberg's creative evolution. He reached that milestone, one year before the première of the *Gurre-Lieder,* with *Pierrot Lunaire,* in 1912. From this point on, "song-speech" would become a major tool of atonal composers whether they wrote songs or operas.

Pierrot Lunaire is a work for "song-speech" and instruments in which twenty tone poems by Albert Guiraud (in a decadent, symbolist style) are set to music so abstract that, in spite of the text, the music is entirely free of any extra-musical connotations. It was almost as if Schoenberg were writing music for words whose context had no meaning for him, so little kinship existed between words and the atonal music.

In Guiraud's poems, Pierrot becomes the symbol of man's varied moods, whims, desires, and emotions. The mood, whim, desire, or emotion is suggested by the title of each poem, such as "Moonstruck" (with which the composition opens) and "Oh, Olden Fragrance" (with which it ends). If the poems are obscure in their symbolic meanings, what can one say about the music? The instrumental accompaniment seems to have a life of its own, independent of the voice, just as the voice appears to be independent of the text. At one or two points, the instrumental background is even the very opposite in connotation from the text. In "Serenade," for example, the words tell of Pierrot playing a viola with a grotesquely long bow, but the instrumental accompaniment calls not for a viola but a cello. Pierrot is then described as plucking on the strings of his instrument, but the cello, in the instrumental background is played with a bow. There is in the words and music of this work a remoteness, a strangeness, a tantalizing obscurity, at times even actual absurdity. In "Outrage," Pierrot bores a hole into a skull which he then fills with Turkish tobacco, following which he smokes the skull as if it were a cigar.

In *Pierrot Lunaire* we encounter a style, sounds, and a manner of vocal writing that shook the foundations of music, so weakening its overall structure that once the collapse of the structure took place, Schoenberg stood ready to build a new one of his own that defied all past rules of design and architecture.

Pierrot Lunaire aroused the fury of both audiences and critics at its première in Berlin on October 16, 1912. There were hisses and shouts and screaming insults from the auditorium. When some of Schoenberg's followers tried to quell the noises, fist fights ensued. "Arnold Schoenberg may be either crazy as a loon, or he may be a clever trickster who is apparently determined to cause a sensation at any cost. His *Pierrot Lunaire* is the last word in cacophony and musical anarchy." This was the report sent into New York by Arthur M. Abell. The knowledgeable and usually tolerant American critic, James Gibbons Huneker, described this as music of "depravity, ugliness, of base egoism, of hatred and contempt, of cruelty. . . . If such music-making is ever to become accepted, then I long for Death the releaser."

Another riot exploded when Schoenberg's atonal first *Chamber Symphony* was given—in Vienna on March 31, 1913. Here is how a correspondent for the *Musical Courier* of New York described the event: "It occasioned the greatest uproar which has occurred in a Vienna concert hall in the memory of the oldest critics writing. Laughter, hisses and applause continued throughout a great part of the actual performance of the disputed pieces. . . . The police were sought and the only officer who could be found actually threw out of the gallery one noisemaker who persisted in blowing on a key for a while. But this policeman could not prevent one of the composers from appearing in the box and yelling to the crowd, 'Out with the baggage!' Whereat, the uproar increased. Members of the orchestra descended from the stage and entered into the spirited controversy with the audience."

But far from discouraging Schoenberg from writing as *he* felt—and not as his audiences and critics demanded—he continued to grow increasingly rebellious and iconoclastic with each succeeding work.

For another brief period (in 1911) Schoenberg was back in Berlin where he lectured on aesthetics at the Stern Conservatory and taught composition at the Akademie für Kunst. He hoped to find in Berlin a climate more agreeable to his *new* music, but in this he was thoroughly disappointed. Then on the eve of the outbreak of World War I he returned to the city of his birth. There, during the war, he taught composition in a school he founded in 1915. Then, until October 1917, he served in the Austrian army.

He wrote little music during the war, but did a good deal of self-evaluation, self-analysis, and theorizing about what he had accomplished in music and where his new methods were leading him. This was the time during which he arrived at a new truth for himself as a composer.

Before we come to the new musical truth to which Schoenberg progressed after concentrating on atonality, we should consider the composer who became the first to attract world attention in his use of both atonality and "song speech." He was Alban Berg, Schoenberg's pupil and disciple, to whom goes the historic distinction of having written the most famous atonal opera in the regular repertory of many major opera companies—*Wozzeck*.

Berg was eleven years younger than his teacher. Born in Vienna on February 9, 1885 to well-to-do parents, he showed a greater interest in literature than in music during his boyhood days. This is the reason why he received no formal musical instruction until his early manhood. He was a sickly boy, suffering as he did from chronic bronchial asthma. And to make matters still worse for him, sickness was ultimately joined by poverty with the death of his father. Possibly as an escape from his physical, psychological, and material problems, Berg now took to writing some music —songs and piano duets—without having had a single music lesson. But music apparently proved little solace. When he was eighteen he tried unsuccessfully to commit suicide— some say because he failed his high-school examinations, others believe that he was the victim of a frustrated love affair.

He seemed to find a new lease on life when first he met Arnold Schoenberg. This was in 1904, when Berg was nineteen. The compositions Berg showed Schoenberg apparently impressed the older man enough to accept Berg as a pupil without fee. Studying with Schoenberg over a six-year period proved a cataclysmic experience for Berg. It gave his life purpose and meaning. To support himself, Berg worked as a government official from 1905 to 1908. Then a small family inheritance enabled him to surrender all outside activities and concentrate solely on music. Berg now completed his first three works to carry opus numbers: the Piano Sonata, Op. 1 in 1908; the Four Songs, Op. 2, in 1909; and his first string quartet, Op. 3, in 1910. In all of this music the influence of both Mahler and Wagner was obvious.

Berg's studies with Schoenberg ended in 1910. A year later Berg married Helene Nahowski, and in 1912 he produced his first work to absorb Schoenberg's revolutionary ideas and techniques: the *Five Orchestral Songs*, Op. 4

(1912), a composition that created a scandal when performed for the first time in 1913, in Vienna. The unusual, even quixotic text Berg chose for these songs was messages which a Viennese poet named Altenberg used to send his friends and enemies on postcards.

Only two more works left Berg's none too prolific pen before the outbreak of World War I, in both of which Schoenberg's atonal style was adopted. They were *Four Pieces,* for clarinet and piano, Op. 5, in 1913, and the *Three Orchestral Pieces,* Op. 6, in 1914.

When war came, Berg tried to enlist in the Austrian army, but was turned down because of his poor health. To aid the war effort he joined the War Ministry as a civilian worker. So disappointed was he that he could not serve his country more actively that he could not summon the will to write music. The war years, then, were a period of creative silence. But, as far as his artistic development was concerned, those years were not wasted. For it was during this time that he came upon a remarkable play by Georg Büchner, *Wozzeck,* which had been written in or about 1836 and published in 1879—an extraordinary work in that its style and mood and writing anticipated the expressionist drama of almost a century later. Berg was completely taken with this strange, haunting drama and became convinced that this was ideal material for the atonal style and the "song-speech" to which he was now so completely dedicated. During the war he worked on the text. Once the war ended he labored long and hard upon his music, which he completed by 1920.

There are perhaps only a handful of operas in the twentieth century where text and music are so ideally mated in spirit and style as they are in *Wozzeck.* The text tells the story of frustrated love, murder, and death through a series of sequences in which the characters and the events have the kind of distortions we encounter in bad dreams, where the subconscious of the characters plays an important role in their behavior, where a strange feeling of unreality permeates the entire somber tragedy. Wozzeck is a poor, downtrodden, and much abused soldier in love with Marie. But Marie favors the drum major. When Wozzeck finds Marie with a pair of earrings which the drum major has given her, he violently accuses her of being unfaithful. Then Wozzeck goes off to settle with the drum major, who gives Wozzeck a sound beating. Now Wozzeck is consumed by anger as well as jealousy. He induces Marie to take a walk with him and stabs her fatally near a pond. He comes to his favorite inn to lose himself in drink. Suddenly he remembers he has left the murder weapon behind him. He returns to the scene of the crime, recovers the knife, and throws it into the pond. Then when he jumps into the water to retrieve it, he drowns. The opera ends poignantly. Children are playing in the street, among whom is Marie's little son, who is riding a hobbyhorse. They hear about Marie's death and rush off to investigate. Marie's son remains behind, enjoying himself as he rides his hobbyhorse, totally oblivious of the fact that his mother is dead.

Atonality, discords, "song-speech" prove ideal musical materials with which to treat this ghastly tragedy. Books can and have been written analyzing Berg's complex and unique score. We must satisfy ourselves here with only one or two examples of how text and music become one and inextricable. There is first of all the unforgettable murder scene. The accompanying orchestra here is a discordant orgy in perfect accord with the gruesome action taking

place on the stage. Then there is the scene in which Wozzeck comes to the pool to search for his incriminating
weapon. The music for this latter episode consists of two
solo violins whispering a ghostly subject of discordant
chords over the atonal squeals of violas playing tremolando
on the bridge of the instrument. To the late Ernest Newman, one of England's greatest musicologists, this music is
"the perfect, the inevitable realization, technical, pictorial
and psychological, of the grisly horror of the scene." And
then there is the deeply moving and dramatic way in which
"song-speech" is used in scenes like the one in which Marie
sings a lullaby to her son; or the one where Marie, in reading the Bible, finds in the story of Mary Magdalen elements
of her own life. All in all, to continue with Newman's
penetrating analysis of this opera, *Wozzeck* is remarkable
for the "unique oneness of the dramatic situations, the
psychology of the characters and the musical expression.
The first of these two elements is so consistently irrational
that a certain irrationality (as the ordinary listener con-
ceives it) in the music also seems right. . . . The non-technical listener . . . finds himself, perhaps for the first time in
his life, taking a vast amount of non-tonal music and not
merely not wincing at it but being engrossed by it."

But a criticism such as this and the engrossed fascination of audiences of which Newman speaks were not encountered when *Wozzeck* was staged for the first time: by
the Berlin State Opera on December 14, 1925, after 137
rehearsals. "I had the sensation," reported Paul Zsorlich
in the *Deutsche Zeitung,* "of having been not in a public
theater but in an insane asylum. On the stage, in the stalls
—plain madmen." In Prague, a year later, there was such
violent opposition to the opera that the police had to order

the management to remove it from the repertory eighteen days after the première.

Like all truly great art, the ultimate victory of *Wozzeck* was inevitable. Because the opera was so provocative in theme and treatment—and because it aroused such violent reactions and so much publicity—performances were by no means lacking. Leningrad produced it in 1927, Vienna in 1930, and Philadelphia and New York in 1931. By the time of World War II, *Wozzeck* had been mounted hundreds of times in most of the major European opera houses. The full recognition of its greatness can be said to have come after World War II, when repeated performances both in America and Europe inspired among audiences ovations instead of riots, and among critics the most rapturous praises instead of contempt.

But let us return to Schoenberg. As he began penetrating ever deeper into the world of musical abstraction —discords, atonality, and "song-speech"—he came to the conclusion that what he had achieved was not full freedom of expression but anarchy. As a creative artist he now needed some kind of order or discipline to keep his imagination in check. He realized that he required some set of new principles to replace the old and unserviceable ones he had discarded. Thus he advanced from atonality to the twelve-tone system (or dodecaphony), the technique with which his name will always be associated and which had the impact of a hurricane on twentieth-century music.

Most people think he invented this system. This is not so. That distinction must go to a little known and rarely performed Viennese composer, one of Schoenberg's contemporaries: Josef Mathias Hauer (1883–1959). Hauer, too, had been an ardent admirer and was profoundly influenced by the expressionist paintings of Kokoschka. In the early 1910s, Hauer developed a new precise system in music based on patterns formed from twelve notes, none of which could be repeated within that pattern. Hauer named this system "tropes," and first used it in *Law,* a piece for the piano, in 1912. Hauer continued writing in this trope method from then on. In 1921 he completed a text explaining his method. Since Schoenberg did not write his first piece of twelve-note music until 1923, it is obvious that the use of the twelve-tone row is obviously Hauer's invention. To his dying day, Hauer remained a thoroughly embittered and broken man because the world looked upon the twelve-tone technique as Schoenberg's creation while he himself was either totally ignored or unknown.

Although the idea of a twelve-tone pattern was born with Hauer, he had failed to gain recognition because his compositions used the system rigidly, unimaginatively, with little suggestion of its true creative potential. Not until Schoenberg took it in hand for his own music and went on to develop it creatively, did the system become a technical device of the first importance.

Schoenberg's first experiment with the twelve-tone system is found in the last number of *Five Pieces for Piano* and in the fourth movement of his *Serenade,* for seven instruments and baritone, both of which came in 1923. His first work constructed entirely in the twelve-tone method was the *Suite,* for piano, in 1924. From then on, for the next two decades, the twelve-tone technique became the creative tool with which he erected a series of compositions that made him the foremost musical revolutionary of his time and opened for music a completely new world of sound values. The most important of these Schoenberg works were the String Quartet No. 3 (1926); the *Variations for Orchestra* (1928); the opera, *Moses and Aaron* (1932); the *Violin Concerto* (1936); the String Quartet No. 4 (1936); *Ode to Napoleon,* for speaking voice, piano, and string orchestra (1942); the Piano Concerto (1942); and *A Survivor from Warsaw,* for narrator, men's chorus, and orchestra (1947).

And now the time has come to ask: What is the twelve-tone system?

It is based upon the twelve notes of the chromatic scale. You can identify those twelve notes by playing all the white and black keys on the piano consecutively beginning with any note. What the twelve-tone composer does before beginning to work on a piece of music is to arrange a definite order of the twelve notes (or as it is called a "row") in which no note is repeated. The reason why it is important not to repeat a note is to avoid any semblance of a melody by assigning to each note the same degree of importance in the row—while in any melodic phrase certain notes have greater significance than others. Once the composer has drawn up his row, beginning on any note he wishes and using the other eleven notes in any sequence he desires, he has the sole subject matter from which his entire composition is built, be it a piano piece, song, symphony, or opera. The entire composition represents a restatement of this one series of tones, but in four different ways. It can be used in its original form as described above. It can be used backwards ("retrograde"), a method by which the composer devises a new row by using the last note of the original sequence as the first note, the penultimate note as the second note, and so on, reversing the order of this original row step by step. A third method is known as "inversion." Here the composer uses his original row, but if the interval between his first and second note is, say, an ascending third, in the inverted method it becomes a *descending* third—in other words the intervallic structure of the original row is reversed. The fourth and final method is retrograde-inversion. Method No. 2 (the backwards or retrograde method) and Method No. 3 (the intervals of the original row being reversed step by step) are combined.

Since a composer can transpose any of the above four series of rows to any step of the chromatic scale—in other words, if he begins on the note C, he can begin another presentation of the four series of rows on a new note, say C-sharp or B-flat, in short in any order of the chromatic scale he desires—this way he has acquired forty-eight ways of using his row.

Schoenberg pursued the twelve-tone method for many years with inflexible rigidity as if it were a mathematical formula; as inexorably as if it were a logical syllogism; as exactly as if it were a slide-rule computation. Though he used this technique with the most extraordinary skill, there was something almost awesomely forbidding in his careful calculations; and the sounds he produced were ugly to the ear and unresponsive to the emotional senses. Gone are the passions, the flame, the intensity of *Transfigured Night* and the *Gurre-Lieder*. Gone, too, the dramatic power and expressiveness of *Pierrot Lunaire!* Schoenberg's twelve-tone compositions were the creations of a highly analytical brain that handles problems of compositions the way a mathematician uses equations, dispensing completely with heart and human experience. Schoenberg might say (as he once did) that a twelve-tone composer, like any other composer, may be "cold-hearted and unmoved as an engineer . . . or may conceive in sweet dreams, inspiration. What can be constructed with these tones depends on one's inventive faculty." But for a long time Schoenberg himself remained hardly more than an extraordinary engineer, not somebody capable of conceiving in sweet dreams and inspiration. He had removed himself completely from the world around him. His insularity was matched only by his intellectualism. He took the body of music and stripped it of flesh, muscle, heart, and pulse, leaving it just a skeleton. All former concepts of pleasing melodies, well-sounding harmonies, euphonious polyphony, thematic development, and variations were thrown into discard. In Schoenberg we had a procession of notes producing a stark atmosphere, a seemingly disorganized structure, baffling in complexity. Even well-trained musicians sympathetic to his aims discovered they were admiring his work with mind and not with heart.

Schoenberg had this to say about the complexity of his writing and its total separation from emotion and human experience. "My music must be listened to in the very same way as in any other music. Forget the theories, the twelve-tone method, the dissonances, and so forth, and may I add: if possible, try to forget the composer, too. I once said in a lecture: 'A Chinese poet talks Chinese but what does he say?' To this I add: It is my own private business to write in this or that style, to use one or another method—this should be of no interest to the listener. But I do want my mission to be understood and accepted."

From 1918 to 1933, Schoenberg divided his year between Mödling (a Viennese suburb) and Berlin, Germany, where he helped raise five children. Two came from his marriage to Mathilde Zemlinsky. One year after Mathilde died, in 1923, Schoenberg remarried. His new wife was Gertrud Kolisch, sister of a famous violinist who had founded and was the first violinist of the Kolisch String Quartet. With Gertrud, Schoenberg had three more children.

In Vienna Schoenberg spent some of his time teaching private pupils, and some running the Society for Private Performances. The latter was an organization dedicated to performances of the compositions of Schoenberg and his circle. Only those who were sympathetic with his ideals were invited, but they were not allowed to applaud or show any other sign of approval when a composition had been played. All critics were barred from these concerts.

In Berlin, in 1925, Schoenberg became professor of composition at the Prussian Academy of Art in succession to Ferruccio Busoni. This was a lifetime appointment, despite which it was suddenly terminated when the Nazis came to power in Germany in 1933. The German Ministry dismissed Schoenberg from his post because he had been born a Jew.

The rise of the Swastika over Germany in 1933 had a tumultuous effect on Schoenberg the man, and eventually on Schoenberg the composer. No longer could he disregard the world outside his own solitary island of musical intellectualism. The bestiality of the concentration camp; the methodical destruction of human rights; the crematories in which human beings were systematically burned to cinders —all this in the land that had produced a Beethoven and a Goethe among other intellectual and creative geniuses— shook Schoenberg to the roots of his being.

He could stay in a German-speaking world no longer. In

May of 1933 he went to Paris where he immediately went through the formal ceremony of being reinstated into the Jewish faith. Now that Hitler was determined to wipe out the entire Jewish population of Germany, Schoenberg could no longer remain divorced from the race into which he had been born and which he had renounced in childhood.

His next move was to withdraw from Europe completely. On October 31, 1933, he came to the United States, which would remain the country of his adoption for the remainder of his life. He Anglicized his name from Schönberg to Schoenberg, and began to study the English language painstakingly. By April 11, 1941, his break with Germany became complete when Schoenberg became an American citizen.

Life was not easy for him in the new world, new surroundings, with new friends and colleagues—and with no money. He drew a pittance teaching at the Malkin School of Music in Boston, hardly enough to support his family. He was in poor health, the victim of chronic asthma.

In 1934, he left the East to make his home in the Brentwood section of Los Angeles, in a modest Spanish-type house within enclosed grounds to protect his privacy. Here he spent the last years of his life. The bulk of his income (and it was not considerable by any means) came from his post as professor of music, first at the University of Southern California, then at the University of California in Los Angeles. He held the latter position between 1936 and 1944. After 1944 he managed to make financial ends meet by teaching a select few pupils, supplemented by the niggardly pension endowed him by the University of California in Los Angeles, by the now increasing royalties from performances of his compositions, which were becoming more frequent, and by royalties from the publication of his works.

Living permanently in the United States, having made such a painstaking effort to forget his German past and become an American, returning to the race of his birth, and the shock and horrors that were transpiring not only in Germany but also in his native Austria—all this had a profound impact on the kind of music Schoenberg was now writing. He was now impelled to remove his art from its one-time total isolation.

To make his compositions a brilliant application of his musical aesthetics and theories—that and no more—could no longer satisfy him. He could no longer worship the cult of abstraction. Now he was compelled by his inner torment to bring to his writing some of the overflow of his profound feelings. Without deserting the twelve-tone technique he was able to produce several works that drew their subject matter for the first time from what was happening to the world around him, and what had happened to him in particular. He would bring emotions to his discords, dramatic thrust to his disconnected tones, programmatic meaning to his twelve-tone row.

In 1939 he wrote *Kol Nidrei,* for speaker, chorus, and orchestra. The *Kol Nidrei* is a prayer for the eve of the Day of Atonement when the Jew expiates his sins committed during the preceding year. Was Schoenberg here expiating his own sin—that of once having deserted his religion? This may very well be the reason why in this, his first *musical* return to Judaism, he should have selected the *Kol Nidrei* as the prayer to set to music.

In 1942 he wrote the *Ode to Napoleon,* for speaker,

piano, and strings. This is a setting of Byron's poem denouncing autocracy in general and Napoleon in particular, while singing the praises of George Washington as a symbol of freedom. This was Schoenberg's first work with political implications, just as the *Kol Nidrei* was his first with religious connotations. By writing music for the Byron poem Schoenberg was voicing, in no uncertain terms, his own contempt for tyranny and dictatorship.

In 1947 Schoenberg completed perhaps his most personal, most deeply felt, and most moving piece of music: a six-minute cantata for speaker, men's chorus, and orchestra entitled *A Survivor from Warsaw*. Like the *Kol Nidrei* and the *Ode to Napoleon*, this work was in strict twelve-tone technique. But flesh and heart and pulse had finally been restored to the skeleton to which Schoenberg had once reduced music in his twelve-tone works.

The inspiration for this remarkable work was the heroism of the Jews of Warsaw when—hungry, sick, hopeless, and equipped with only the most rudimentary military weapons—they held the Nazi war machine at bay for weeks. These Jews had for a long time been herded by the Nazis into a Warsaw ghetto where they lived under the most appalling conditions; at regular intervals, groups were removed for extermination in concentration camps. When the ghetto population had been reduced to 40,000, the Jews decided to resist. That resistance began on April 19, 1943. With a courage little short of Herculean, those Jews withstood an uninterrupted attack from the tanks and machine guns of a large disciplined army, standing grim and firm behind their ghetto walls, killing as many Nazis as their primitive weapons allowed. The men, women, and children of the ghetto were determined to die rather than submit to surrender. This resistance, which by all military logistics should have ended in a single day, if not in a few hours, lasted almost a month. By May 16, 1943, practically every Jew in the ghetto was dead, except for a negligible handful which somehow had managed to escape through an underground passage, and another handful that were still alive when the Nazis finally were able to storm through the walls.

The work opens with an agonized outcry in the orchestra (the twelve-tone series fixed in two chords of six notes each). A descending voice of despair is raised by the cello. This leads immediately into the opening line of the spoken text—the work of Schoenberg himself, written in English except for the concluding Hebrew prayer. The speaker begins: "I cannot remember everything. I must have been unconscious most of the time; I remember only the grandiose moment when they all started to sing, as if prearranged, the old prayer they had neglected for so many years—the forgotten creed! But I have no recollection how I got underground to live in the sewers for so long a time."

And now the speaker proceeds to describe what had transpired behind those ghetto walls on the final day when the Nazis finally penetrated the improvised bastion. The Nazis found that practically all the Jews were dead. To the scattered few still alive, the Nazis screamed hysterical orders, warning them that "in a few minutes I will know how many to send to the gas chamber." Then the tempo quickens, the rhythm accelerates, the mood becomes frenzied. The speaker says: "They began . . . first slowly, One, Two, Three, Four—became faster and faster so that it finally sounded like a stampede of wild horses." This hypertensioned outburst becomes the arch reaching toward the climax of the entire composition. All of a sudden a male chorus (representing the remnants in the ghetto) voices the prayer closest to all Jewish hearts: "Hear, O Israel, the Lord Our God, the Lord is One." Though spoken in Hebrew, this part is in "song-speech" with no Hebraic identity in the music. It is not a prayer here. Schoenberg had no intention of creating Hebrew music. He was producing a human document. This is a moment in music that can turn stone to water.

Listen to the terrifying intensity of emotion of this music and ask yourself if the twelve-tone technique has not finally proved its artistic validity; if the background to the text of those individual, scattered tones drawn from the twelve-tone series and the austere, disconnected sounds do not express a sorrow and a terror that stab the heart more sharply than a blade. Through the techniques and methods and mannerisms developed over the years in working with twelve-tone compositions, Schoenberg manages to compound tension upon tension, futility upon futility, terror upon terror, despair upon despair.

A Survivor from Warsaw meant a good deal to Schoenberg—not only for its poignant message and its description of a historic event that had so stirred the heart of the composer. It is more than possible that this work represented to its creator a symbol of his own life and work following the Nazi rise in Germany and its occupation of Austria. Before 1933, Schoenberg had been hiding within a ghetto of his own making—an intellectualized musical ghetto. He had finally emerged from it into the blazing sunlight, to return to the race he had rejected in childhood, to rejoin humanity which he had kept out of his personal creative world for most of a lifetime and for which he had held such contempt. His intellectual solitude, his insularity had once and for all been shattered—just as the walls of the Warsaw ghetto had crumbled. But he proved more fortunate than those Jews who had been trapped in that ghetto. Their fate was death. Schoenberg's fate was greatness—greatness and immortality.

Schoenberg lived only about four years after writing *A Survivor from Warsaw*. Those of us who met him on and off during that period recognized a change in the man, as well as in the artist, in his last years. Before 1947, and shortly thereafter, his bitterness against audiences, critics, musicologists, the music world in general had become so rigidly encrusted that it was impossible for him to find satisfaction within himself that finally, in the middle 1940s, he had become recognized as one of music's giant pioneers. His seventieth birthday, in 1944, stimulated nationwide tributes and all-Schoenberg concerts. To the sponsors of these events—as well as to many of his friends—Schoenberg despatched the following acidulous comment: "For many years I have resigned myself to the fact that I cannot hope for a full and appreciative understanding of my work—for what I have to say as a musician." He concluded by saying that a true recognition of his contribution could come only after his death.

In 1947, the National Institute of Arts and Letters gave him a Special Award of Distinguished Achievement. His response was to send the Institute a stinging letter in which he venomously denounced all those who attacked him for years and years. The Special Award, he said, should have rightfully been given to his numerous enemies since it was they who brought him worldwide attention—notoriety instead of fame, malice in place of appreciation. When in 1948 the distinguished Nobel Prize winning novelist, Thomas Mann, published *Doctor Faustus*—a novel whose central character is a composer of twelve-tone music—he was considerate enough to print an introductory statement explaining that "the twelve-tone system is in truth the intellectual property of a contemporary composer and theoretician, Arnold Schoenberg" and that "passages of this book that deal with musical theory are indebted in numerous details to Schoenberg's *Harmonielehre*" (a treatise on harmony Schoenberg had completed in the 1910s). Schoenberg's reaction? Dr. Mann had stolen "my literary property . . . ascribing my creation to another person which, in spite of being fictitious, is represented as a living man." Schoenberg insisted that future generations would consider Thomas Mann as the creator of "my theory."

But a softening process began to take place in Schoenberg after 1948. The continuing growth of his fame and influence had finally succeeded in cracking the hard outer layer of his personality. When the city of Vienna paid him honor with various tributes he accepted them gracefully, and with gratitude. He even spoke of returning to Vienna. He enjoyed having his friends visit him, all of whom were welcomed warmly; he found joy in playing with his grandchildren and his houseful of pets; he took such delight in the parties his wife and children gave him on his birthdays that he often entertained them with witty parodies of popular Viennese songs. The bitter man, in short, had become mellow.

He did not live to return to the city of his birth, just as he did not live to complete his opera *Moses and Aaron*, two acts of which he had composed in 1932. At that time he had abandoned the work, and did not return to it until 1951 the year of his death. He wanted desperately to write the third act, the text for which was already finished, because he regarded this Biblical opera as his masterwork. Based on sections from the *Exodus,* Schoenberg's libretto begins in Egypt with the voice in the burning bush calling on him to save his enslaved people. The climax of the second act is an orgy before the Golden Calf. Moses becomes the symbol of spiritual ideas, his brother Aaron, the representation of the "doer." Schoenberg wanted to end his opera with the victory of spirit over action, Moses over Aaron. The entire opera is based on a single twelve-tone row with the part of Moses spoken while that of Aaron is sung or declaimed. Song-speech plays an all-important role in the musical style.

Arnold Schoenberg died in Brentwood, California, on July 13, 1951. Though Schoenberg died without writing the third-act music, *Moses and Aaron* has been widely performed in its incomplete state: first over the Hamburg Radio on March 12, 1954; then staged in Zurich on June 6, 1957; after that in several of the world's leading opera houses. It was produced in the United States in Boston on November 30, 1966.

Hans F. Redlich, writing in *Opera News,* called *Moses and Aaron* a "tremendous religious experience. When the music ebbs away prematurely at the end of Act II—with Moses despairing of his vocation in a moving passage combining instrumental melody and song-speech—an artistic and human experience has reached its consummation, which may well represent to future generations the musical high-water mark of the century."

And so, what Arnold Schoenberg had foretold back in

1912 has come true. "The second half of the century," he had said, "will compensate by excessive praise for the lack of understanding that my work received in the first half of the century." One may take exception to the word "excessive" in this prophetic sentence. But nobody today will deny that Schoenberg's music and Schoenberg's theories have by now been thoroughly vindicated. He, too, was the voice of tomorrow's music.

The human equation Schoenberg brought to his twelve-tone writing in the *Ode to Napoleon* and *A Survivor from Warsaw,* the dramatic intensity that pervaded his use here of his formerly cut-and-dried mathematical system—these had been anticipated by his pupil-disciple, Alban Berg. For long before Schoenberg did so, Berg succeeded in bringing to twelve-tone music such emotional and ardent responses that he came to be known as the "romanticist of the twelve-tone school."

Berg proved that the twelve-tone system could be lyrical as well as emotional and romantic. He first proved this in his appropriately entitled *Lyric Suite* which, in 1926, was written for string quartet, but three movements from which Berg later transcribed for chamber orchestra. Only half of the six movements of this string-quartet suite is in the twelve-tone technique—but even those in a dodeca-phonic style are intensely emotional in character. The atmospheric or emotional content of each of the movements is revealed in the tempo markings. The first movement is *Allegretto joviale* (or "jovial Allegretto"). In the same way, descriptive words are appended to the tempo markings of the other movements as follows: "amoroso" (loving), "misterioso" ("mysterious"), "appassionato" ("passionate"), "dilerando" ("delirious") and "desolato" ("desolate"). So human does Berg become in this ultramodern music that he even essays a passage in the style of a Viennese waltz in the second movement. Erwin Stein, a noted authority on the twelve-tone "school," regarded the fourth movement as "a summit of lyric expression through broad melody." In the final movement Berg (for reasons never explained) briefly quotes from the Prelude to Wagner's *Tristan and Isolde*—perhaps in a moment of happy recollection of years past when Berg had esteemed Wagner so highly to the point of imitation.

While only half of the *Lyric Suite* is in the twelve-tone technique, Berg's Violin Concerto is entirely in that system. Here, as in the *Lyric Suite,* Berg permits himself the luxury of allowing his heart as well as head to dictate the kind of music he was writing. This Concerto is one of the three or four greatest such works for the violin in the twentieth century—and there are some violin virtuosos who even consider it the greatest of all. Certainly it is an unqualified masterwork.

It was commissioned by Louis Krasner, a concert violinist, in 1934. Since Berg was then deep at work on a huge twelve-tone opera, he might never have come around to writing the concerto but for the fact that early in 1935 he was emotionally stirred by the death of a young girl, Manon Gropius, the daughter of a dear friend (Gustav Mahler's widow by a second marriage). This death inspired him to produce a work in her memory, and the commissioned concerto provided him with an opportunity to do so. The concerto has two movements. The first (where the main theme, presented by the solo violin, is built from the twelve-tone row) was intended as a portrait of the girl. A recurring interval (a perfect fifth) serves to symbolize the girl's purity. Joyous music follows in this movement, some of it carrying reminiscences of Viennese dance music—for here the composer remembers the girl when she was full of the joy of life and the bloom of youth. The second movement is dramatic and tragic, for now Berg must speak of her death. The death struggle is portrayed in a violin cadenza. Death stalks through the music in figures for the horn. The music achieves a high point of intensity before it comes to rest with a quotation from a chorale by Johann Sebastian Bach (*"Er ist genung"* from the cantata, *O Ewigkeit*). This is a token of resignation in the face of the inevitable. From then on the music becomes a most poignant elegy.

Louis Krasner introduced the concerto in Barcelona on April 19, 1936, when the late Constant Lambert, distinguished English composer, conductor, and critic, called it "the most beautiful and significant piece of music written since the war [World War I]." It has subsequently been performed by most of the world's famous violinists and on several occasions has been recorded.

The opera Berg was working upon when he interrupted this task to write his violin concerto was *Lulu* which, tragic to say, he did not live to complete even though he had spent seven years on it. This is the only other opera by Berg besides *Wozzeck*, but where *Wozzeck* was an atonal opera, *Lulu* is entirely in the twelve-tone technique. Like *Wozzeck*, however, *Lulu* is a musical drama of shattering power, filled with both grief and pity. Its text (like that of *Wozzeck*) was prepared by the composer himself, the source this time being two dramas by Frank Wedekind, the distinguished German realist playwright (1864–1918). The leading character, Lulu, is a sordid, disreputable, vicious woman who brings to their death several men involved in her life, who serves a term in prison after having murdered one of them, and who ends up as a prostitute and is murdered by Jack the Ripper. A more repulsive character has probably never crossed the opera stage. But to both Wedekind and Berg, Lulu was just a symbol of the sordid passions, frustrations, and the capacity both for self destruction and the destruction of others which hides latent in most human beings.

Few studies of the character of Lulu, and the way she was treated by Berg, are as revealing as one by a Prague critic who, regrettably, cannot be identified since his criticism was not signed. He wrote: "Lulu is a heroine of four dimensional power in her endurance and her suffering, destroying all that she magnetizes. She is a phenomenon of nature, beyond good and evil, a complete cosmos whose secrets, altogether removed from ordinary comprehension, can be revealed only by the music. The way this glowing ball of fire scorches everybody that it touches and finally burns itself out, leaving all life about it extinguished or fading away, has led the metaphysician in the composer to make the transposition to those unearthly spheres, where figures flicker in death like dream images, illumined only by the last dying afterglow of a great irresponsible drama."

The twelve-tone row appears without preliminaries in the opening measures of the score. From then on Berg adheres to the principles and methods of the twelve-tone system with almost the inflexibility of his teacher, Schoenberg. Notwithstanding this fact, the opera is filled with music that has compelling passion and drama, and at moments (in some of the dance rhythms) even lightness for contrast.

Berg completed only two acts, 268 measures of the third act, and the finale of his opera. When *Lulu* received its world première—in Zurich on June 2, 1937—the opera was given exactly the way Berg had left it. But in many subsequent presentations, including the American première in Santa Fé, New Mexico, on August 6, 1963, the third act was filled out with spoken dialogue lifted out of Wedekind.

From the beginning of its performance history, *Lulu* has been highly acclaimed. Leading critics in both Europe and America have not hesitated to describe it as a "masterpiece," as "one of the epochal achievements of twentieth-century opera," and as a work that "will endure as long as opera itself will." One other indication of the high regard with which this opera is held is the fact that two full-length recordings were released almost simultaneously (naturally in performances by two different companies) and both have been commercial successes.

Alban Berg's premature death (which had made it impossible for him to finish his opera) came about through blood poisoning caused by a bee's sting. Just before he died he had the hallucination that he was conducting a performance of *Lulu*. He cried aloud: "Upbeat! Upbeat!" He never did live to see a stage performance of this opera. But at the last concert he was able to attend he had heard a presentation of an orchestral suite derived from *Lulu* at a symphony concert in Vienna. This was only thirteen days before his end came on December 24, 1935.

Anton Webern

(1883–1945)

From the handful of pupil-disciples who had clustered around Arnold Schoenberg in Vienna, who had listened to each of his words as if it were gospel, who had worshiped him as man and teacher, and who had thoroughly assimilated his ideas and technique, there emerged one man who progressed a step beyond Schoenberg in developing the twelve-tone system. That step was a giant forward stride toward tomorrow's music.

This composer was Anton Webern. The development he brought about was to amplify the twelve-tone system into what eventually came to be known (when fully crystallized) as "serialism." The impact of serialism since 1950 proved even more decisive than Schoenberg's twelve-tone system had been. Strange—is it not?—that it is Webern, of all other dodecaphonists who were directly influenced by Schoenberg, who should today be most widely honored, most widely performed, and most widely recognized as the prophetic musical voice of our new music. For Webern was almost never performed while he was still alive. Few anywhere knew what he was writing, or for what goal he was aiming. His elevation to world acclaim by an entire generation of avant-garde composers of the post-1950 period was something that occurred long after Webern met his untimely, tragic death. So famous and influential has Webern become that he has even succeeded in throwing Schoenberg and Alban Berg into a secondary position among the avant-gardists. We now know that the great twentieth-century revolution in music, in which some of the sounds of tomorrow were evoked, has Webern for its point of departure—as Pierre Boulez and Karl Stockhausen, among other present-day musical revolutionaries, have attested.

Webern was the descendant of a titled family that owned an estate in the Carinthian district of Austria since the nineteenth century. At the time of his birth (in Vienna on December 3, 1883), and for many years thereafter, he was called Anton von Webern. He preferred dropping the designation of nobility, "von," from his name late in life.

His father was a mining engineer who could well afford to give Anton, and Anton's brother, a thorough academic education. Anton went to schools in the Austrian towns of Graz and Klagenfurt, following which, in 1902, he entered the University of Vienna from which he received a doctorate in music four years later, having studied musicology with Guido Adler. Webern's earlier musical training had begun in 1893 in Klagenfurt with Erwin Komauer, with whom he had studied piano, cello, and theory.

The discovery in 1961 of a cache of Webern's manuscripts revealed that his career as a composer had begun much earlier than we had thought. This "find" contained several songs (completed in 1898, when the composer was fifteen). It also included other early Webern compositions unknown even to authorities of the twelve-tone school: a ballad for voice and large orchestra, *Siegfried's Sword,* written in 1903, for example, and *Summer Wind,* a work for large orchestra completed one year later. What is most interesting about these early works is that they betray that the young Webern—even as the young Schoenberg had been before him—was both an admirer and an imitator of Wagner. These compositions abound with Wagnerian chromaticisms, Wagner-type orchestration, and the sensual and dramatic elements that Wagner had stressed. And the title, *Siegfried's Sword,* obviously springs out of Wagner's *The Ring of the Nibelungs* in which Siegfried's sword plays so dominant a part in the text.

Between 1904 and 1908 Webern studied with Schoenberg. Schoenberg was, as we have already remarked, himself then undergoing a radical transformation which carried him away from Wagner and toward atonality. Along this new path, Schoenberg led his pupils, all of whom followed him meekly and without questioning. Webern was one of them.

Webern's last work linking him with the Romantic past was the *Passacaglia,* for orchestra, Op. 1 (a passacaglia being a form similar to a theme-and-variations, popular with instrumental composers of the Baroque era, including Johann Sebastian Bach). But if one foot of Webern stood in the past, the other rested in the future. The main theme on which these variations are based is not a sustained melodic thought—as it had previously been in traditional passacaglias—but a mere fragment of an idea (played in unison and in octaves). Henceforth, Webern would grow increasingly partial to fragmentary themes. Another later Webern method that can be discovered in this *Passacaglia* is the use of broad leaps in the intervals of his fragmentary themes.

Beginning in 1909, Webern's break with the musical past became complete and permanent. In *Five Pieces for Quartet,* that year, Webern walked at Schoenberg's side into the undisciplined, disordered world of atonality. After that, Webern wrote the *Four Pieces,* for violin and piano, and the *Six Pieces,* for orchestra, both in 1910; the *Five Pieces,* for orchestra, in 1911; and the *Six Bagatelles,* for string quartet, in 1913.

However much Schoenberg directed Webern's musical writing and thinking, Webern was a creative personality in his own right. From his beginnings he developed his own mannerisms to which he would cling for the remainder of his life. One of the things in which Webern believed most strongly was brevity. He was convinced that true musical wisdom—like so many good things—came in small packages. Nobody before him achieved his kind of concentration. All of the *Six Pieces,* for orchestra, for example, take only five minutes to play; the fourth piece consists merely of 6 1/3 measures. All of the *Six Bagatelles* comprise only forty-eight measures; the shortest of these has but eight measures.

And if Webern insisted upon saying what he had to say as succinctly and as quickly as possible, he also made a fetish of the Schoenbergian goal to achieve musical abstraction by reducing his means, materials, and ideas to their basics while dispensing with all nonessentials. A theme had to be a mere fragment. A composition had to consist of nothing more than a series of such fragments—no development, no variation, no repetition, and as little harmony as possible. "Once an idea has been stated," Webern said, "it has expressed everything it has to say. A composer has to go on to his next thought." For example, the first of the *Six Pieces*, for orchestra, begins with four low notes in solo flute. After that we hear one note in muted trumpet, two chords on the celesta, four notes on the flute, one note in French horn, and so on. The series of fragments are pieced together into a mosaic consisting merely of brief, seemingly unrelated sounds. "A whole novel is expressed in a single sigh," is the way Schoenberg described one of these fragments. Very often each note in a fragment is assigned to a different instrument. "They are melodies in one breath," explained Erwin Stein. As one tone is given by one instrument, a second tone by a second instrument, a third tone by a third instrument, what we get is a new concept of what a theme should be: not a series of tones making up a melody, but a procession of tones creating a spectrum of rapidly changing colors.

Hand in hand with brevity, concentration, and the reduction of musical means to the barest essentials, came understatement. Webern liked to write music that whispered rather than shouted, that maintained as low a scale of dynamics as was possible. His sonority in the *Five Pieces*, for orchestra, is reduced from *pianissimo* to almost inaudible sounds. (In the entire work there is only one change in dynamics—a single measure that ends the second piece in something just above a whisper.)

Up to the time he had completed the string-quartet *Bagatelles* in 1913, Webern had been employed as a conductor of theater orchestras in various German and Austrian cities over a five-year period. This was the time when he got married: to Wilhelmine Mörtl, in 1911, with whom he had four children.

When World War I broke out, Webern enlisted in the Austrian army. He did not wear his uniform long. His defective eyesight, from which he had long been suffering, brought him release from military service, much against his will. He now went to Prague where he earned his living conducting orchestral concerts. Then, after the war ended, he returned to his native land, making his home in Möd-ling, a suburb of Vienna, not far from Schoenberg. His relationship with Schoenberg now became a closer one than that of pupil and his teacher, a disciple and his men-tor. Webern became one of several ultramoderns who helped Schoenberg found in Vienna the Society for Private Musical Performances (discussed in the chapter on Schoen-berg).

Webern was never a prolific composer. He averaged about a work a year—a remarkably small output when we remember how spare and short his compositions were. Starting with *Three Spiritual Folk Songs,* for voice, violin (or viola), clarinet, and bass in 1924, he began employing the twelve-tone technique, but without deserting his own passion for a simplicity that seemed almost naked when compared even to Schoenberg's music.

Writing did not come easily to Webern. That concentra-tion, compression, economy, understatement we find even in his twelve-tone compositions were the result of the most painstaking revisions, deletions, and editing. A single note often cost him hours upon hours of concentrated thought before he decided that that was the note that would serve him, and none other.

Above and beyond the labor pains he expended upon

even the slightest details of each composition, Webern had to sacrifice a good deal of his precious time to the necessary business of earning a living for his family. Between 1922 and 1934 he conducted the Workers' Symphony Concerts in Vienna; in 1928, he led the Workers' Chorus; and in 1927 he was appointed director of the Austrian Radio. During these years he also made occasional guest appearances as conductor in several European cities.

A commission from the League of Composers in New York (a society dedicated to the promotion of new music) led Webern to write his only symphony, in 1928. This is an epoch-making work. It is here that Webern, using the twelve-tone technique, extended its horizon by suggesting the possibility of using this technique for elements in music other than pitch. Besides, it is in this work that Webern achieved what is probably the ultimate in abstraction. The tones stand in total isolation from one another. Sometimes a single tone becomes Webern's entire theme. There is no varying sonority, very little harmony, the barest suggestion of a rhythmic pattern. There are even times when no sound is heard at all, the sound texture being broken up by continual rests. "Their bare bones," said René Leibowitz of this music, "frighten us."

Many critics and progressive young composers of today regard this Webern symphony as possibly the most influential composition of the twentieth century, although it would take another two decades after 1928 for these young composers to use Webern's method as the point of departure for their own innovations and developments. The Webern Symphony is not only a new language with a new vocabulary, but a new structure, a totally new concept of what music can and should be.

But when the Symphony was first heard anywhere—in New York in 1929—it represented to its listeners sheer chaos. "What the audience heard," said Oscar Thompson, the critic, "suggested odd sounds in an old house when the wind moans, the floors creak, the shades rustle, and the doors and windows alternately croak and groan." Another critic, Samuel Chotzinoff, compared the sounds of this music to those "uttered at night by the sleeping inhabitants of a zoo." A third critic—Olin Downes—maintained that this Symphony was the perfect fruition of futility.

But Webern, like Schoenberg, was neither shaken nor depressed by such reactions. In his subsequent works he continued further along the procedures he had crystallized in his Symphony. He knew that *he* was right and that his critics were wrong. And he was confident that time would provide the necessary proof of his belief. "In fifty years at the most," he exclaimed, "everyone will experience this music as *his* innate music. Yes, even for children it will be accessible. People will sing it."

And he was not far from wrong, though we are still some distance from the time children will be singing Webern's kind of music. The world in general has come around to Webern's thinking—unfortunately, after his tragic death. A half century following his bold, self-assured prophecy, a Webern society sprang up with branches in eleven countries. Beginning with 1961, there took place Webern festivals in Seattle (Washington), the famous Salzburg festival in Austria, in Buffalo (New York), and at Dartmouth College. Columbia Records released an album containing *all* of Webern's works, which (considering how esoteric this commodity was) had a surprisingly large distribution. On the twentieth anniversary of Webern's death, plaques were placed on the house where he died and on the church in which his body lay. Two different ballets have been inspired by Webern's music: *Episodes* (choreography by George Balanchine) and *Moments* (produced by the Harkness Ballet).

But what is perhaps most significant is that Webern became the inspiration for young progressive-minded composers all over the world—not only composers of serious music but even composers of jazz (this latter type of popular music becoming known as "progressive jazz"). The serious composers imitated Webern, then extended and amplified his methods. That extension, that amplification in time came to be known as "total organization"—or, more popularly, "serialism." Serialism is the twelve-tone technique carried to its ultimate possibilities. I shall explain this technique in greater detail in my next chapter, on Pierre Boulez.

The tragedy that first touched, then overwhelmed, and finally destroyed Webern began in 1933 when the Nazis rose to power in Germany. Webern was not Jewish, but to the Nazis his music represented "cultural Bolshevism." This is the reason the German government did not allow Webern's music to be either published or performed in that country, cutting off a source of Webern's income which, however small it may have been, represented an important addition to the small sums he could command as a teacher of private pupils. When the Nazis took over Austria, Webern's formerly pitiable financial plight was further depleted. His poverty, however, was only one reason for his rapidly mounting melancholia and inner rage. Another was the fact that the two composers most sympathetic to his work were no longer capable of bringing him encouragement and solace. One of them was dead (Alban Berg). The other (Arnold Schoenberg) was in America. "Yes, my dear fellow," Webern wrote to one of his colleagues in 1939, "things have taken a turn quite different from what we expected."

But Webern's troubles were only just beginning. The outbreak of World War II first brought heartbreak, then doom. Heartbreak was caused by the death of his son during a bombing attack. Doom arrived with the murder of Webern by an American soldier because of mistaken identity.

As an escape from the ravages of war, Webern and his family sought refuge in a humble, almost shabby, abode in the little town of Mittersill, in the Austrian Alps. He and his family lived there in appalling poverty. Webern's troubles had been responsible for the disintegration of his health: He was suffering continually from disorders of the stomach but did not have the price for proper medical treatment. Nevertheless, he did not stop writing music. This was his sole escape from the gruesome realities of the world around him and his tragic personal life. He completed two cantatas for soprano, bass, chorus, and orchestra between 1940 and 1943.

In 1945, American troops occupied Mittersill; this was soon after Nazis Germany had surrendered to the Allied forces. On the evening of September 15, 1945, Webern was smoking an after-dinner cigar while strolling outside a hut occupied by his daughter and son-in-law. An American sentry espied him, and called out to him to stand still. Webern did not understand the soldier's command and kept on walking. The sentry shot him with a fatal bullet. . . .

At least this is the story that was long circulated and believed for about fifteen years after Webern's death. Then an American scholar, who had an exalted admiration for Webern's music—his name is Hans Moldenhauer—decided to go to Mittersill to investigate the truth of Webern's death. The facts he uncovered were far different from those that had so long been accepted.

Webern's son-in-law was involved in black-market operations. When this came to the notice of the American authorities, they despatched two soldiers to arrest the offender. It just happened that on this very evening Webern had been invited to his daughter's home for dinner. As a special treat, the son-in-law gave Webern one of the cigars he had acquired illicitly. Webern, of course, knew nothing about his son-in-law's black-market dealings. The soldiers arrived at the home of the son-in-law at 9:45 in the evening, just as Webern was outside the house enjoying the pleasures of his cigar to the full. One of the two American soldiers mistook Webern for the son-in-law, and suspecting that his prisoner was trying to escape, fired at him. Webern staggered into the house whispering "It is finished." Only then did the soldier realize he had killed the wrong man. So tormented did this soldier become by his disturbed conscience that later he became a chronic alcoholic, which, in turn, brought about his premature death.

Webern dead? Physically, yes. Creatively, he was destined to become increasingly alive and vital as the years passed. As the father of serialism he belonged not to music's past but to its future. It was Webern—and not Schoenberg— who led one of our modernists (Ernest Krenek) to say that

Webern's music represented the most revolutionary break with the established traditions of music in all of music history; that inspired Pierre Boulez to maintain that anything written before Webern was obsolete; that inspired a brilliant young American composer, Gunther Schuller, to create a new technique baptized "third stream" (consisting of the marriage of the rhythms and improvisations of jazz with serialism).

Pierre Boulez

(*1925–*)

To most music lovers Pierre Boulez today is perhaps best known as a conductor, a career that reached its zenith when, in 1969, he was made musical director of the BBC Symphony in London, and even while holding down this all-important post, succeeded Leonard Bernstein in 1970 as the musical director of the New York Philharmonic. World recognition for Boulez's achievements on the podium has tended to obscure his creative accomplishments, which have been hardly less formidable. For Boulez has been one of the basic forces in the revolution separating the music of yesterday from that of tomorrow. He stands in the vanguard of those post-World War II innovators working with new techniques. That of Boulez is serialism, the roots of which are embedded in the soil of the Webern symphony discussed in the last chapter.

Boulez came upon the idea of serialism from the fact that in his symphony Webern often used a different instrument for a different tone until each instrument had been heard from. Thus the application of the twelve-tone technique to tone color was realized. And if the twelve-tone technique could serve, first, pitch (with Schoenberg and Alban Berg) and then tone color (with Webern), why could it not also be applicable to other elements of music? Thus argued Boulez.

To keep the historic record accurate, we should point out that virtually at the same time that Boulez evolved and made world-famous the technique of serialism, an American composer, Milton Babbitt, was also working in the same direction. In 1946 Babbitt explained the technique in a monograph, *The Function of Set Structure in the Twelve-Tone System,* the first theoretical work ever written about serialism; and between 1946 and 1947 Babbitt embodied this theory in two compositions—*Three Compositions,* for piano and *Compositions for Four Instruments,* the latter receiving a citation from the New York Music Critics' Circle.

Today we are inclined to associate Babbitt much more with the development of electronic music (particularly with music for the synthesizer) than with serialism. And we tend to single out Pierre Boulez, rather than Milton Babbitt, as one of the first major serialists because his work has had such a profound impact on musicians everywhere.

The time has arrived to explain what serialism is and in what way it differs from Schoenberg's twelve-tone system.

Serialism is the twelve-tone technique applied to musical elements other than pitch. In planning a composition, serialists select not only a twelve-tone row which becomes the basis of the thematic and harmonic pattern of the entire work; serialists use the twelve-tone method to govern dynamics, rhythm, timbre, and so forth. Serialists, for example, select twelve different note values (quarter notes, half notes, sixteenth notes, and so on) and do not repeat a note value until the other eleven have been used. In the same way, serialists formulate twelve different dynamic markings, articulations, tone colors, rhythms—once again using one of each without repeating it until the other eleven in each category have been heard from. Thus serialists aimed at "total organization" where Schoenberg and Berg and even Webern had achieved only "partial organization." More than ever before, music was to be conceived with the exactitude of mathematics.

The first significant use of serialism took place in 1948 with Pierre Boulez's *Piano Sonata No. 2*. This, Boulez has explained, was "the decisive step towards an integrated serial work, that will be realized when serial structures of tone colors and dynamics will join serial structure of pitch and rhythm." "Powerful, almost totally dissonant," is the way the critic of *The New York Times*, Harold C. Schonberg, described the Boulez sonata, "full of wildly leaping figurations and compositional complexities, it was just what was needed to set off the stampede into the post-Webern style of writing."

In France, the première of Boulez's sonata created a furor of arguments and denunciations not only from the more conservative diehards in French music, who insisted that music was now being reduced totally to set formulas and therefore had completely abolished creativity, but even from Schoenberg's followers, who considered anybody who digressed from their master's system as a heretic. But if Boulez was fiercely attacked for his first use of serialism, he was also soon to find followers and believers in his new method. From the 1950's on, the list of composers embracing serialism as their principal compositional method is a formidable one.

Pierre Boulez was born in Montbrison, a French town in the department of Loire, on March 26, 1925. A musical prodigy, he not only received music instruction in his childhood from teachers in nearby St. Étienne, but was also a member of the church choir in his native town. His teachers were continually amazed at his sure musical instincts, and the rapidity with which he absorbed what he was taught. But Boulez's father, an industrialist, had other ideas: he insisted that Boulez become an engineer. And so, after attending a preparatory school in Lyons, Boulez was sent to Paris to attend there the Polytechnical School.

This was the time of World War II. In spite of the war, in spite of the Nazi occupation of Paris, there took place in Paris at that time a considerable amount of musical activity. The making of music was encouraged by the Nazis as one way of pacifying the Parisians, and was accepted eagerly by the Parisians who found in music a refuge from the grim events of the times. This varied and highly significant program of musical events so stimulated Boulez that he soon deserted the idea of becoming an engineer and returned to music study: initially, the piano with Andrée Vaurabourg (the wife of one of France's major composers, Arthur Honegger); then harmony with Olivier Messiaen, another all-important creative voice in French music. Messiaen had highly original ideas about the importance of rhythm in music. He had made an extensive study and use of not only the most complex rhythmic patterns and procedures of the Western world but also the even more complicated rhythms of East Europe and the Orient. The young

Boulez became taken with his teacher's fascination for rhythm. After being graduated from Messiaen's harmony class in 1945, clutching first prize in his hand, Boulez continued to study composition with Messiaen for about a year. Messiaen having now become his inspiration, Boulez completed his first compositions, two works which concentrated on intricate rhythmic structures: *Three Psalmodies,* for piano, in 1945, and a Sonatine, for flute, in 1946.

But a new and even greater musical stimulus than Messiaen had begun to arouse Boulez in 1945: the twelve-tone technique, to which he had been introduced by reading *Schoenberg and His School* by René Leibowitz. Convinced of the validity of this system, Boulez became Leibowitz's pupil that year. Leibowitz converted Boulez into a thoroughly confirmed twelve-tonalist. Boulez now felt that this was the way a composer could free himself once and for all from all past Romantic associations, by adopting a creative process controlled by a predetermined method. "Since the discoveries by the Viennese," Boulez now said, "all composition other than twelve tones is useless." And so, in 1946, he produced his first works in the Schoenberg technique: two sonatas, one for solo piano, the other for two pianos.

It was not long before Boulez began feeling that the twelve-tone system had possibilities far greater than those posed by Schoenberg. Boulez wished to impose even greater control on his creativity, and thus divorce himself completely from all past musical practices. And so he completed his Piano Sonata No. 2, and serialism emerged.

Boulez has remained a faithful serialist (for the most part), though he often wandered off to other experimental fields of creativity, such as electronic music, and music of chance. One of his most famous works is *The Hammer Without a Master (Le Marteau san maître)*, written between 1953 and 1954, and introduced in Baden-Baden, Germany on June 18, 1955. This is a nine-movement work for contralto and six instrumentalists (one of the instrumentalists is required to play ten percussion instruments, including bongos, maracas, tambourines, bells). The text consists of three poems by René Char that creates sometimes sensitive, sometimes abstract impressions rather than amplifying any specific theme. Three of the movements are these three poems set to music; the other six movements, all instrumental, provide tonal commentaries on the poems that had been sung. The nine movements are divided into cycles of three movements each—one movement sung, two movements played by the instrumentalists. The three cycles of three movements, the composer suggests, can be played in any order the performers wish.

This composition, entirely in serial technique, calls for rapidity of motion, generally high pitches, themes that are just fragments, continual changes of tone color and dynamics and rhythm, and often delicate and unusual sound effects produced by such more or less exotic instruments as the xylorimba (a cross between the xylophone and the marimba), the vibraphone, and the guitar. Despite the complexity of Boulez's music and the obscurity of Char's poems, the combination of music and words creates at times an exquisite, at times a dramatic, at times a highly atmospheric or esoteric effect to which some audiences have responded enthusiastically and which has sent many a sophisticated music lover to the shops to purchase the Columbia recording of this work.

The poetry of Stéphane Mallarmé was the stimulus for

two highly important Boulez compositions. One is *Pli selon pli*, for orchestra, which Boulez intended as a portrait of the poet. The other is the *Three Improvisations on Mallarmé*, for voice and orchestra. Mallarmé was a French Symbolist poet who was more interested in aural sounds of words than in their meaning. His poems were studied attempts to liberate poetic writing from any kind of expressivity, to the point where his poems are often virtually incomprehensible. This was a goal with which Boulez could sympathize completely. Boulez, too, wanted to free music of expressivity. "The goal of music," he has said, "is far richer than that. . . . Music must give a sense of mystery." Before composing *Pli selon pli* (a task consuming five years) Boulez took one of Mallarmé's volumes of poetry, tore out the pages, then assembled his text by taking only those pages he found useful. Boulez explained that the structure of the poems in his text—the form, the meter, the order, and the sound of the words—were translated by him into musical terms according to advanced serial principles. The result was a work of extraordinary power as well as originality.

In *Three Improvisations on Mallarmé* Boulez introduces the element of chance by permitting the female voice to improvise the musical material for the Mallarmé poems. In the rest of the composition the orchestra performs the serial music as Boulez had written it down on paper.

Still another poet, Henri Michaux, inspired a work in which for the first time Boulez experimented with electronic music. This composition is *Poetry for Power (Poésie pour pouvoir)* which comprises, on the one hand, musical sounds recorded on tape and, on the other, music performed live by two orchestras. Thus electronically produced music is set into opposition to music produced by orchestral instruments. Here the serial method produces, as Ernest Thomas has noted, "different results when one applies the same serial organization to a tempered tonal system, namely that of instrumental music, from those it produces when one applies it to the universe of non-tempered electronic sonorities." Thus Boulez further extended his serial writing by borrowing the new resources of which electronically produced music is capable. "In *Poetry for Power*," continues Thomas, "the two elements, instrumental and electronic, are sometimes opposed and sometimes combined. The text of the poem binds the two elements but not in the form of primitive blendings. The word, recited on tape and through loud-speakers—the language sound—is submitted to structures in the melting pot of electronic processing, so to speak, so that the language of sound becomes part of the universe of sound."

While evolving his new musical language and establishing himself as a world figure in avant-garde music, Boulez supported himself between 1948 and 1958 by conducting the orchestra in a Parisian theater. There, of course, he was required to work with the conventional kind of music from which, as a composer, he was trying to divorce himself completely. If his conscience troubled him that, to make a living, he had to involve himself as conductor with music for which he had little sympathy, it became placated in 1954 when he initiated a series of avant-garde concerts in Paris. These became annual events, known as *"Domaine musicale,"* where the most revolutionary tendencies in music could find a hearing. Apparently there were audiences for this new music, even large audiences, since the *Domaine musicale* had to move three times from one auditorium to another, each time to find more seating space: from a little theater to the Salle Gaveau, and then to the Odéon Theater. Its historic significance in introducing new music which other French organizations ignored can hardly be overemphasized.

Coincidence rather than calculation first turned Boulez to the conducting of serious new music. This happened at his own *Domaine musicale*. In 1956, a conductor scheduled to lead Boulez's *The Hammer without a Master* became indisposed. Virtually at the zero hour, Boulez had to step into the conductor's shoes. One year later, he once again replaced a conductor—this time one whose work during rehearsals with a Boulez contata so displeased the composer that the latter decided to take over the direction. A number of guest appearances at various modern music festivals in France and Germany threw the limelight on Boulez's instinctive talent and profound musicianship when he stood on the conductor's platform. In 1960 he received his first important conducting appointment with the Southwest German Radio Orchestra in Baden-Baden. He extended his conducting activities during the next few years to embrace the Salzburg Festival in 1961 (where he gave a stunning performance of Stravinsky's *The Rite of Spring*), the Paris Opéra in 1963 (where he brought down the house with his electrifying rendition of Alban Berg's opera, *Wozzeck*), and in America in 1964 where he made his conducting debut with the visiting BBC Symphony, in New York. Later conducting commitments brought him to Bayreuth (in *Parsifal*), Japan (*Tristan and Isolde,* with the visiting Bayreuth Festival company), and as guest conductor of major orchestras in America and Europe. George Szell, music director of the Cleveland Orchestra, became so convinced of Boulez's powers as conductor that he gave him an unprecedented contract: a five-year agreement to appear for several weeks each year with his orchestra. Appointments as music director of both the BBC Symphony (in succession to Colin Davis) and the New York Philharmonic followed.

Because so many of his conductorial assignments had been concentrated in both Paris and Germany, Boulez for a long time maintained two homes: an apartment on the Boulevard Raspail in Paris and a house in Baden-Baden, Germany. Then, in June of 1966, Boulez broke all ties with his native land, gave up his apartment there, and resigned from all French musical organizations with which he had been affiliated, including his successful *Domaine musicale*. What had led Boulez to renounce France was the same kind of fierce integrity and idealism that would allow him to make no compromises whether as a composer, as a conductor of serious music, or as a scholar. What had happened was that in 1966 the French government had created a new bureau in the cultural ministry, placing at the head of its music division a musician who, besides being a comparative reactionary where music was concerned, was also in Boulez's estimation, a musician of inferior capabilities. To place a third-rate musician to superintend all the musical activities in France seemed to Boulez a disgrace to his beloved art, and this he would not tolerate. As a token of defiance, Boulez refused to have further traffic with the land of his birth. Considering how much Boulez has accomplished and how highly the civilized world esteems him, the loss Boulez suffered in renouncing his country is minor when compared to that sustained by France, deprived of one of her greatest musicians. The cliché here holds true: a prophet is not without honor save in his own country.

Most of the post-Webern twelve-tonalists, convinced of the validity of Boulez's innovation, graduated into serialism, including Hans Werner Henze, Alberto Ginastera, Luigi Nono, Witold Lutoslawski, Karlheinz Stockhausen, Luciano Berio, Leon Kirchner, Ernest Krenek, among others.

A comparatively recent opera in a basically serial technique has won the accolades of critics. It is *Don Rodrigo* by the Argentine composer Alberto Ginastera (1916–   ). It opened the new home of the New York City Opera at the Lincoln Center of the Performing Arts on February 22, 1966, and proved the unquestioned highlight of the City Opera season. Harold C. Schonberg, critic of *The New York Times,* called it a "stunningly impressive work that is going to be in the opera repertoire for a long time." Previously, when this opera had been given its world première (in Buenos Aires on July 24, 1964), John Vincent called it "a landmark similar to *Wozzeck.*"

Don Rodrigo, text by Alejandro Casona, has for its hero the last of the Visigoth kings whose defeat at the battle of Guadalete in the eighth century was responsible for the downfall of Spain. Don Rodrigo's ruin had come about because he had dishonored Florinda, daughter of the governor of Ceuta, who then sent his troops into Spain and defeated Rodrigo's army. Rodrigo escapes to a monastery in search of penance, where he is followed by Florinda in whose arms he dies.

This comparatively simple but highly effective and at times poignant text is matched by music which makes extensive use of "song-speech" and atonality as well as the serial technique. The opera does not leave audiences with melodies to remember, but with a theatrical experience not soon forgotten.

The progress from a Schoenbergian and Alban Bergian twelve-tone style to a Boulez serialism is a natural development on the part of composers like Ginastera who have long aimed in their work for control and organization. Startling, however, was the conversion of Igor Stravinsky to serialism so late in his career, placing him in his late years solidly in the camp of the post-Webern avant-gardists. Of course Stravinsky—who long ago established his world reputation as an undisputed master in twentieth-century music—had been a rebel almost from his beginnings as a composer. His career is now too well known for us to indulge in biographical details here. But certain phases of his creative life should be mentioned to explain why the world of music was shaken to its foundations when he turned serialist.

He had been no novice at shaking the foundations of the music world. Born in Oranienbaum, near St. Petersburg, in June 17, 1882 (the son of a famous opera basso), he was initially strongly affected in his musical writing by Russian music (by Glinka, Tchaikovsky, and his own teacher, Rimsky-Korsakov, particularly) before he launched his first major attack against tradition and orthodoxy. After producing a number of works of negligible interest, all of them obviously derivative of those Russian composers he admired, Stravinsky became affiliated as composer with the Ballet Russe, then recently founded by Sergei Diaghilev. For the Ballet Russe, Stravinsky produced between 1910 and 1917 a series of strikingly provocative ballet scores in which his own personality became clearly identified: scores filled with discords, polytonality, complex and rapidly changing rhythms and meters, dislocated accents, orgiastic sonorities. All this represented a radical departure from past practices in music, so much so that a new movement was here brought into existence: "Neo-primitivism," in which the power and dynamism of primitive music—with its emphasis on rhythm —were encased within sophisticated structures. Beginning with *The Fire-Bird (L'Oiseau de feu)* in 1910, and continuing with *Petrouchka* in 1911, *The Rite of Spring (Le Sacre du printemps)* in 1913, *The Song of the Nightingale (Le Chant du rossignol)* and *The Wedding (Les Noces)* in 1917, Stravinsky became one of the most provocative, most fiercely criticized and (with the musical youth of his time) the most imitated of composers. The world première of his *The Rite of Spring* caused the greatest scandal in French contemporary music, with such a riot and hubbub within the theater that nobody could hear the music. Time, however, has provided perspective. Today there are not many to doubt that each of the compositions mentioned above is the work of one of the most original creative figures in the music of the 1910's; each is now recognized as a masterwork.

Then, after having established himself as the leading musical rebel of his time with his primitive style, Stravinsky suddenly turned about-face to enter a new creative phase in which, instead of being the voice of the future, he suddenly became an apostle of the past. Once again he was to start a new movement in music that first caused shock and controversy, which then profoundly affected the direction many composers around the Western world would henceforth take, and which finally was accepted as a major forward step in Stravinsky's artistic growth. His new movement was "neoclassicism," a return to simplicity, objectivity, clarity, lucidity, economy—and to the structures of the past. This new trend represented for Stravinsky a total rejection of the style that had previously made him both famous and notorious.

After a period of transition between 1917 and 1923—when a number of works such as *The Story of a Soldier (L'Histoire d'un soldat)* and *Pulcinella* provided a clue as to where Stravinsky was beginning to head—he wrote an Octet, for wind, in 1923 in which his neoclassic style became fully crystallized. There followed concertos, symphonies, various other works for orchestra, ballet scores, choral music, and the opera *The Rake's Progress,* in which for over a quarter of a century Stravinsky proved himself the completely dedicated neoclassicist.

The Rake's Progress was written in 1950 when the composer was sixty-eight years old. In this highly significant and widely performed opera (text by W. H. Auden and Chester Kallmann inspired by engravings by Hogarth), Stravinsky was profoundly influenced by the classical operas of Handel, Gluck, and Mozart, to the point of using the operatic structure favored by those masters (arias, duets, ensemble numbers, finales, and so forth) and employing a harpsichord to accompany the recitatives as had been habitual in the eighteenth century. Few of those who were so enchanted with this delightful period piece were aware that with it Stravinsky was using his neoclassic style for the last time. For, once again, Stravinsky felt impelled to reject the methods, the musical ideology, and the style that had produced masterworks. It was impossible to guess at that time (even had we known that Stravinsky was creating a permanent break with his neoclassic past) that his new (and

last) creative phase would embrace first the twelve-tone system and after that serialism. For Stravinsky had long and
heatedly denounced these techniques.

Then, without warning, Stravinsky startled the music
world a third time by writing the *Cantata on Four Poems
by Anonymous English Poets* (1952) in which he used
the twelve-tone technique sparingly and only in random
passages. Once he had put his toe in the waters of twelve-
tone music, he proceeded to put one foot in: with his
Septet in 1953. Twelve-tone music apparently did not
completely satisfy him—but serialism did. In 1956 he completed a religious work, the *Canticum sacrum,* written in
honor of St. Mark, patron Saint of Venice. This seventeen-
minute work was Stravinsky's first in an entirely serial
method. So eager was Stravinsky to have his audience comprehend his new creative manner that when it was introduced in Venice on September 11, 1956, he had the piece
played twice, before and after the intermission.

From then on one ambitious serial work followed another: religious works, a Biblical spectacle for TV, works
for solo voices with or without chorus but with orchestra,
a sacred ballad, and the *Variations* for orchestra (1965) that
was used by George Balanchine as background music for
a ballet. Even some of Stravinsky's most ardent admirers
were taken aback by his new music. Now that they had
come to recognize the greatness of his neoprimitive and
neoclassic works they were puzzled to find their master, in
his old age, not only entering but permanently occupying
the strange world of serialism.

Stravinsky has been subjected to a good deal of severe
criticism for his last works (just as he had been fated to
encounter denunciations when he wrote his first neoprimi-

tive compositions, and later his first neoclassical works). But as he has often complained, the public has always refused to keep step with him "in the progress of my musical thought." He said further: "What moves and delights me leaves them indifferent and what still continues to interest them holds no further attraction for me. For that matter, I believe that there was seldom any real communion of spirit between us. . . . Their attitude certainly cannot make me deviate from my path. I shall assuredly not sacrifice my predilections and my aspirations to the demands of those who, in their blindness, do not realize they are simply asking me to go backwards."

In his old age Stravinsky is still moving forward. He, and not his severest critics, had been right when he was so convinced in the past of the truth of his musical message in presenting the world with giant works like *Petrouchka* and *The Rite of Spring* and *Oedipus Rex* and the *Symphony of Psalms,* and his best concertos and symphonies and *The Rake's Progress.* He is just as convinced today that the path of serialism is the inevitable one for him to pursue. It may very well be that although his serial works have thus far failed to equal the popularity of his earlier masterpieces, once again he and not his critics is right—that time will prove it so, just as it has done in the past.

| *He brought noises into music.*

Edgard Varèse

(1883–1965)

You hear the shriek of a siren, the piercing scream of a jet plane, the outcries of automobile horns, the nerve-tingling slamming of a door—and hundreds of other noises that have become basic to our way of life. And you shudder.

On the other hand there are now composers who find that noises such as these, and many others as well, have a definite and important place in the musical art; that there is music in noise; that noise is as basic to contemporary musical writing as it is to contemporary life.

Such composers are convinced that no longer must music be organized and calculated with such long-accepted materials as scales, tonalities, harmony, counterpoint, melody, following the accepted laws of acoustics, and put down on paper in traditional musical notation. These new composers believe that music can be disorganized, can dispense with the materials mentioned above, need no longer be annotated in the long-accepted manner, but calls for a new kind of notation consisting of parabolas, diagrams, designs, curves, spherical figures.

The first important innovator to use noise as a creative process was a French-born American, Edgard Varèse. Like every prophet, he was the object for derision and annihilating criticism in his own time; and like every other such visionary he has come to be recognized by many of our avant-garde composers as a prophet.

However, the interpolation of noise in a musical composition was not new with Varèse. Great composers of the past experimented with noise effects, sometimes to achieve realism, sometimes for comic effects. Christoph Willibald Gluck wrote a composition for drinking glasses containing different amounts of water and thus producing different tones. Mozart used real sleigh bells in one of his German dances. In one of his overtures, Rossini had the violinists tap their music stands with the wood of their bows. Mahler used cowbells in a symphony. Richard Strauss manufactured a wind machine for a tone poem, and a thunder machine for a symphony—in each instance for the purpose of simulating noises produced by natural phenomena.

In 1913, Luigi Russolo, an Italian futurist composer, issued a manifesto explaining the necessity of bringing noises into music. "Life in ancient times was silent," he wrote. "In the nineteenth century, with the invention of machines, noise was born." He added: "We must break out of this narrow circle of our pure musical sounds and conquer the infinite variety of noise sounds." To prove his thesis, he conceived of an orchestra made up of six groups of implements capable of creating noises mechanically—whistles, screams, percussion noises, the voices of animals, and so forth. One of his compositions required a man to imitate the sound of snoring.

In 1916, the eccentric French composer, Erik Satie, wrote the score for a remarkable ballet, *Parade,* where the orchestration included the actual clicking of typewriters, the sound of whirring roulette wheels, sirens, the hum of airplane motors. While Varèse was already experimenting with noises in music, Ravel used a cheese grater in the orchestra for his stage fantasy, *The Child and the Sorcerers (L'Enfant et les sortilèges),* producing a unique non-musical effect he was seeking to accompany the stage action. A year or so later, George Antheil, a young American, shocked audiences in Paris and New York with a composition entitled *Ballet mécanique (Mechanical Ballet),* requiring the services of automobile horns, anvils, machines, player pianos, and various kinds of percussions not generally encountered at symphony concerts. Antheil explained that his work was not intended to glorify machines (though it was planned to speak for a machine-oriented society) but to interpret "the barbaric and mystic splendor of modern civilization—mathematics of the universe in which the abstraction of the human soul lives." When the *Ballet mécanique* was first heard in America (in New York on April 10, 1927) the audience yelled out its disgust at the excruciating sounds. One prankster in the audience lifted a cane to whose end he had attached a white handkerchief —a symbol of surrender; he then proudly marched out of the auditorium while the performance was going on. Later on in his career Antheil abandoned noise-making compositions for those calling for traditional instrumentation, notation, and idioms. But for Edgard Varèse there never was any retreat from his initial attacks on the musical establishment. Indeed, with the passing of years, he grew bolder in his innovations.

Edgard Varèse was born in Paris on December 22, 1883 (*not* 1885, as most biographical dictionaries maintain). His early interests were science and mathematics, studies which he pursued assiduously in Turin. But music also fascinated him. When he was only eleven he wrote an opera, *Martin Paz*, without having taken a single lesson in composition.

His parents wanted him to become an engineer. He was expected to enroll in the Polytechnical School in Paris in 1904. But the young man had a mind of his own. He was now determined to become a musician. For the first time he now undertook the study of music systematically, first at the Schola Cantorum (where his teachers were the renowned composers Vincent d'Indy and Albert Roussel), and after that at the Paris Conservatory (where he became the first student to capture a prize then initiated by the city of Paris—the *Bourse artistique*). Later on, he involved himself further in music-making by founding and directing a chorus and organizing and supervising public concerts.

Though he had been thoroughly trained in the music of the past, and actually became a recognized scholar of the choral music of the fifteenth, sixteenth, and seventeenth centuries, his goal as a composer, from his very beginnings as a trained musician, was to free sound from its ties to the past. Experiments which the scientist Helmholz had made with sirens led him to conceive of a new kind of music made up of "beautiful parabolic and hyperbolic curves," to use his own words, similar to those found in "the visual domain." From then on he knew that some day he would create a kind of music the concert stage had never known.

After spending a number of years in Berlin—conducting, composing, but always toying in his mind with new kinds of musical sounds—and after being rejected from the French army at the breakout of World War I because of bad health, Varèse came to the United States. He remained in America as long as he lived, becoming a citizen in 1926. At first he earned his living conducting an orchestra in New York, the New Symphony, which he himself had founded. He included on his programs so many new works that one year after he had organized his orchestra he was dismissed by its directors. They wanted him to conduct the kind of music audiences favored, but Varèse was thoroughly unconcerned with public taste. He was far more interested in giving contemporary composers a hearing. And so, in 1921, with Carlos Salzedo (a famous harpist, but also a passionate advocate of new music) he formed the first organization in America devoted to modern music: the International Composers' Guild. This group lasted six years, giving the works of more than fifty modern composers, some of which (including music by Schoenberg and Webern) were getting their first hearing in New York.

But besides promoting *new* music, Varèse was also *writing* new music. He now became the seeker after new sounds. As he put it: "I do not use sounds impressionistically as the Impressionist painters used colors. In my music, sounds are an intrinsic part of the structure." At first, Varèse depended upon traditional instruments, usually creating new effects by exploring the extremes in sonorities, combining his instruments in unorthodox ways to produce consistent discords, and emphasizing and carrying to an extreme the rhythmic capabilities of percussion instruments. In 1923 came *Hyperprism,* scored for wind instruments and percussion (the latter including sleigh bells). Olin Downes of *The New York Times* found in this music only the hubbub of "election night," the screams and wails of a "menagerie or two," and the strident outburst of "a catastrophe in a boiler factory."

In 1924, Varèse completed *Octandre*—a "ribald outbreak of noise," as the critic W. J. Henderson described it. An "octandre" is a flower with eight stamens. Varèse's composition was for eight instruments, each seeming to go its own way as far as harmony and tonality are concerned. A monumental discord resulted. New sonorities were continually being uncovered through unusual technical use of the various instruments, individually and collectively. Said W. J. Henderson: "It shrieked, it grunted, it chortled, it mewed, it barked—and it turned all eight instruments into contortionists."

One year later Varèse wrote *Integrales,* for small orchestra and percussion. Varèse's previous indifference to any set structure or form, and his avoidance of any recognizable melody or formal harmonies, took one step closer toward abstraction, while his fascination for outlandish sounds was becoming something of a fetish. He was still searching for new sonorities. Here, said Mr. Henderson, the music at times sounded like "an injured dog's cry of pain or a cat's yell of midnight rage, and sundry instruments of percussion crash and bang and apparently just for the sake of crashing and banging."

Varèse continued seeking out all the possibilities of formal instruments and percussion to create new sounds in two subsequent works for large orchestra: *Amériques* in 1926 and *Arcana* in 1927. When he came to the conclusion that formal musical instruments can go only so far producing new timbres and sound qualities. He now knew he had to work with nonmusical instruments. And so, in *Ionisation,* in 1933, he used two sirens and expanded his percussion section with various instruments of his own invention capable of producing arresting sibilant or friction noises of undetermined pitch. His percussion group comprised no less than forty-one instruments played by thirteen musicians.

Ionisation begins with a *"tambour militair,"* a kind of tambourine, pounding out a few notes as background to the screaming of two sirens and glissandi of two harps, the sounds of the sirens and the harp glissandi going in opposite directions. Then the percussion instruments enter— literally with a bang. Contrasting colors are produced by tapping on or beating special metal and wood objects devised by Varèse, by the ringing sounds of tubular chimes, and by tone clusters on the piano. The pianist bangs out chords by plunging either two fists or both forearms across the keyboard in the lowest register. Noise, as a musical process, had now become fully emancipated.

To Paul Rosenfeld (one of the few critics of Varèse's day able to recognize the importance of these experiments) the sounds of the city became an exciting aural experience because he had heard Varèse's music. "The streets are full of jangly echoes," wrote Rosenfeld. "The taxi squeaking to a halt at the crossroad recalls a theme. Timbres and motives are sounded by police-whistles, bark and moan of motor-horns and fire-sirens, mooing of great sea-cows steering through harbor and river, chatter of drills in the garishly lit fifty-foot excavations. . . . A thousand insignificant sensations have suddenly become interesting, full of character and meaning."

Mr. Rosenfeld wrote further: "Varèse has used his new sonorous medium in interests other than those of descriptivity. He has never imitated city sounds as he is sometimes supposed to have done. . . . He is a musician; and if the auditory sensations of modern life have developed the musical medium under his hands, it is merely because they have sought him out. . . . If his artistic medium has developed and spread under Varèse's hands, it is only because his entire activity is directed toward encompassing the reality of our swift prodigious world in its terms. . . . His high tension and elevated pitch, excessive velocity, telegraph-style compression, shrill and subtle coloration, new sonorities and metallic and eerie effects are merely the result of his development of the search-and-discovery principle in the twentieth-century world."

Having myself become intrigued with Varèse's one-man crusade to transform music into noise, I visited him in the early 1930s at his home on Sullivan Street, in Greenwich Village, where he owned a brownstone house which he occupied with his wife. I expected to find a long-haired Bohemian whose eccentric music would be matched by his eccentric behavior and appearance. Varèse's studio was on the ground floor next to a garden, and it was there that I found him. He was a man of solid build with a huge head crowned with a mass of hair. His eyes pierced through you as he spoke. You did not have to be with him very long to realize that this was no eccentric or charlatan but a profound musician, a man of enormous erudition both in and outside of music. He had come to certain conclusions about music that had been carefully thought out. The existing scales, structures, contrapuntal and harmonic procedures, he felt, were as outmoded as a horse-drawn surrey in the automobile age. Melody and consonance were things of the past. Music had to be freed of all the inhibitions that centuries of tradition and rules had imposed upon it. He never referred to his own works as "musical compositions." He preferred the term "organized sound." The music of the future, he insisted, would consist exclusively of processions of sounds—any kind of sound that comes within man's aural experience. These sounds would be encased within a form that was no form at all, the sound flowing with the utmost of freedom, however, and wherever it wished until the creator had arrived at and fulfilled the aural effects he was trying to achieve. "I try to fly on my own wings," is the way he put it.

Gradually, now one composer, now another—many emboldened by Varèse's experiments—began thinking more and more in terms of noise and noisemakers. In 1927, a Soviet composer, Alexander Mossolov, was inspired by factories to write *Iron Foundry,* for orchestra, in which a metal sheet was shaken to imitate the sound of a machine in motion. A year later George Gershwin used actual taxi horns (imported from Paris) for his tone poem, *An American in Paris.* Still in the 1920s and early 1930s, Nicolas Slonimsky wrote a composition in which a special noisemaker had to imitate the sound of a "cat's meow," while in another work he interpolated the noise made by exploding balloons pricked by pins. Ferde Grofé interpolated the sound of clicking typewriters in *Tabloid.* A composer named Harold G. Davison created a work entitled *Auto Accident* which required the following implements: "Two plate glasses each resting on a wash bowl or crock, with a hammer or mallet, in readiness to smash them." The score then explains: "On page nine, measure four, these plates are to be shattered with the hammer, one on the second count, and the other on the second half of the third count. In the next measure, the bowls containing the broken glass are to be emptied on a hard surface, table or floor."

Nearer our own day, one of England's creative musical giants, Ralph Vaughan Williams, felt impelled to introduce wind noises produced by a special machine in order to re-create realistically the Arctic weather in his *Sinfonia antartica* in 1952. In 1955, Ernst Toch, a Viennese-born American composer, introduced in his Third Symphony noises from a tank of carbon dioxide which made hissing sounds through a valve, and from a wooden box in which croquet balls are set into motion by a rotating tank to create a percussive sound. That this symphony was no mere stunt, and that the use of noise within an otherwise conventional composition had aesthetic value was proved when the symphony captured the Pulitzer Prize for music. The eerie voices of actual whales, reproduced on tapes, were incorporated by Alan Hovhaness (1911–   ), an American composer partial to exotic and esoteric music, in his symphonic work, *And God Created Whales*, whose world première took place in New York on June 11, 1970, André Kostelanetz conducting. (Not Vaughan Williams, nor Toch, nor even Hovhaness can be regarded in any sense as ultramodernists, let alone avant-gardists. Yet even they finally have come around to the awareness that tones produced by musical instruments alone are sometimes insufficient to create the artistic effects they are seeking.) In *Echoes of Time and River,* four "processionals" for orchestra by George Crumb (1929–   ), winner of the Pulitzer Prize for music in 1968, a unique effect is achieved at the end of the fourth movement by the introduction of phonetic sounds: whistles from two groups, one group on the right of the stage, the other on the left. In a later chapter, notably on John Cage, we shall have a good deal more to say about the use of noises in musical creation.

By the early 1930's, Varèse came to the realization that he had exhausted the possibilities of noisemakers, percussive sounds, and unorthodox ways of playing traditional instruments—all for the purpose of creating new types of sonorities. For this reason he decided to write no more. Only when the world of electronics suddenly opened up for him altogether new potentials for the creation of sounds and sonorities (undreamed of before this), would he return to his creative worktable. We shall discuss the evolution of electronic music in detail beginning with our next chapter. Here and now it is only necessary to say that early in the 1930's Varèse became acquainted with a primitive instrument whose tones were produced by means of electricity—the Thereminvox. New timbres, new tone qualities were now available to him. In 1934, he wrote *Equatorial,* in which the Thereminvox was one of his instruments. But the Thereminvox had highly limited capacities, something which Varèse soon came to realize. And so, once again, he lapsed into creative silence, lasting about twenty years.

He ended that silence because after World War II electronics had changed the world—and music as well. Now, through electronics, there were no limits to the density, pitch, quality, and variety of sounds and sonorities that could be produced. Still convinced of the validity of his

concept of "organized sound," Varèse seized upon electronics for his last compositions. "Composers," he said, "are
now able as never before to satisfy the dictates of that inner
ear of the imagination." *Deserts,* for wind instruments,
percussion, and sounds produced on magnetic tape came
in 1954; here Varèse three times interpolated within his
musical context electronically produced noises. Percussion
instruments performing complicated rhythmic patterns
served as the transition from electronic passages to those
for the wind instruments.

Varèse's next work was a giant electronic operation, the
Poème électronique, in 1957, written for the Philips Pavilion at the World Exposition at Brussels. This composition required the use of 425 loud-speakers to project eight
minutes of sound record on tape. This music was intended
to supplement a series of lights flashed on the curved ceil-
ing of the pavilion—though no effort was made to create
any affinity or relationship between music and lights. The
combination of electronic sounds and coruscating colored
lighting proved a stunning aural-visual experience that
drew ovations. Here is how one American critic, Edward
Downes, described Varèse's work: "[It] started with a
sound as of vast church bells tolling. It came from all
sides. . . . There followed sounds suggesting sirens, kettle-
drums, gunshots, skyrockets, exploding into outer space,
and then something like a slowed down human voice
seemed to sigh: 'Oh, god. . . . ,' the pitch of the final vowel
sinking gradually into the bottomless depths of a booming
chamber." When *Poème électronique* was heard in New
York for the first time (minus the lights) it inspired such
an ovation it had to be repeated.

Varèse's last composition was *Nocturnal,* for soprano,

men's voices, chamber orchestra, and electronic sounds. It was written in 1960 and introduced in New York on May 1, 1961. It was part of an all-Varèse program that drew a full house which (after *Nocturnal* had been played) sprang to its feet in homage to the composer.

Edgard Varèse died in a New York hospital on November 9, 1965, following intestinal surgery. Death came *after*, not *before*, his lifework had proved its significance; *after*, not *before*, his fame and reputation had become solidly grounded. By 1960, his work was considered so important that Columbia issued a recording of some of his leading compositions. The all-Varèse concert in which the composer received a standing ovation in 1961 was followed three years later by another all-Varèse program, this time performed by the New York Philharmonic under Leonard Bernstein. Meanwhile, in 1962, Varèse received the Brandeis University Award in Music, while at a dinner in his honor in New York in 1963 he was given the Koussevitsky International Recording Award. In 1965 Varèse was presented with the Edward MacDowell medal for distinguished contributions to music. "One day," wrote Peter G. Davis about Varèse's last composition, *Nocturnal*, though he may just as well be talking about all of Varèse's works since the early 1920's, "composers may equal and even surpass the vision of these remarkable conceptions. Today, however, they are works by which the future must be measured."

Karlheinz Stockhausen
(1928–   )

In the late 1940s, Pierre Schaeffer, a Parisian engineer, inaugurated a new movement in music that has come to be known as "concrete music" *("musique concrète")*. With the cooperation of the Experimental Club *(Club d'Essai)*, a group affiliated with the Paris radio station, *Radiodiffusion française,* Schaeffer began reproducing all kinds of noises on magnetic tape. Then by slowing down or accelerating the speed with which the tape rotated, or combining on one tape the noises recorded on two or more other tapes, he managed to concoct all types of weird noises. Convinced that this material had value as music, Pierre Schaeffer wrote the *Symphony for the Single Man (Symphonie pour un homme seule)* in which the sounds heard by a solitary man during the day, arranged in rhythmic patterns, were reproduced.

It was the influence of "concrete music," to which he first was introduced during a brief visit to Paris, that made

Edgard Varèse return to composition after a two-decade hiatus—with *Deserts* in 1954. "Concrete music" also made an indelible impression upon the brilliant young French musician, Pierre Boulez, who had started out his career as mature composer by using the serial technique and from there went on to exploit electronics.

And it was due to "concrete music" that a new world of musical possibilities opened up for Karlheinz Stockhausen, who was one of the first significant composers of electronic music—and still is.

"Concrete music" was not the real beginnings of electronic music. Experiments with electricity by composers had preceded it by several decades. Among the more important electronic devices interesting composers before "concrete music" came into being were the Thereminvox and the *Ondes musicales,* the latter now known as *Ondes Martenot,* after the man who invented it ("ondes" meaning "waves").

The first, the Thereminvox, was the creation of Leo Theremin, a Russian scientist who, in 1919, was appointed director of the Laboratory of Physico-Technical Institute in Russia. There he created an electronic instrument in which musical sounds were produced by electric oscillations varying in pitch as the movements of the hand approached or receded from the instrument. Theremin first demonstrated his instrument at the Electrical Congress in Russia in August of 1920. In 1927 he toured the United States. Enough interest in the Thereminvox was generated in the United States to impel Leopold Stokowski, then the musical director of the Philadelphia Orchestra, to use it at one of his concerts; for a recital of music for the Thereminvox to be given in New York; for a Russian-born

American composer and theorist, Joseph Schillinger, to write several compositions for it, including his *Airphonic Suite;* for Edgard Varèse to use it in *Equatorial* in 1934; for Miklos Rosza to use it in his background music for two movies, *Spellbound* and *The Lost Weekend,* in order to create eerie effects.

Ondes musicales was the creation of Maurice Martenot, a French scientist, in 1928. This is an improvement over the Thereminvox where electric instrumental tones could be produced only through glissandi—one tone gliding into the next. With *Ondes musicales,* tones could be produced on a keyboard with accurate pitch and without transitional tones. A good many French composers have been sufficiently intrigued by the *Ondes musicales*—or to use its later designation, the *Ondes Martenot*—to write major works for it. Arthur Honegger included it in the orchestration of his masterwork *Joan of Arc at the Stake (Jeanne d'Arc au bucher)* in 1938. Pierre Boulez, André Jolivet, and Olivier Messiaen were three other important French composers to use this electronic instrument. And in America, Samuel Barber used it in the orchestration of his opera *Antony and Cleopatra,* whose world première opened the new auditorium of the Metropolitan Opera Association at the Lincoln Center for the Performing Arts in 1966.

Further significance in the potential of electronic music became evident with the invention of huge electronic machines able to do what no musical instrument performed by humans could hope to duplicate. In these machines, sounds, recorded on magnetic tape, were transmitted through loud-speakers. With the aid of an oscillator (or electric current), the purest tones rid of all overtones could be created. Where music had previously been chained to the limited number of fixed notes, and no more, the electronic machine could create pitches from the lowest to the highest that the ear could possibly detect and absorb (up to 20,000 vibrations). Dynamics could be increased and decreased to points heretofore thought impossible. Equally unrestricted were the qualities of timbre producible, and the duration in which a note or group of notes could be held. What, then, had formerly been a highly circumscribed sphere of musical possibilities had now become limitless, far beyond all previous aural experiences.

The first musician to inaugurate the earliest *significant* laboratory for electronic music was Karlheinz Stockhausen. This happened in 1953 at NWDR, the West German Radio in Cologne where Stockhausen was then employed and where he initiated a Studio for Electronic Music. Actually this was not the first such laboratory. That distinction goes to Werner Meyer-Eppler at Bonn University in 1949; and in 1952 important experiments in electronically produced music were proceeding at Columbia University in New York by Otto Luening and Vladimir Ussachevsky. Meanwhile, the first public performance of electronic music had taken place at Darmstadt, Germany, in 1951.

Nevertheless, it was Stockhausen, more than any other single person, whose work focused the limelight of world attention and interest on electronic music and served to inspire his contemporaries and successors.

Stockhausen is a German composer who began his career by writing music for traditional instruments in a more or less accepted way until he came to the conclusion that what he was creating expressed neither himself nor his times. This music, he sensed, was outmoded stuff. He was bored with both writing and listening to the kind of music that everybody else had been producing for generations. But he had to pass through a number of important influences and experiences before he could beat out a path of his own, and to travel to places on whose ground composers before him had never stepped.

Karlheinz Stockhausen was born in Mödrach, near Cologne, Germany, on August 22, 1928. He began his musical training early and continued it intensively for many years. Between 1947 and 1950 he studied the piano with Hermann Schroeder at the High School of Music in Cologne; from 1950 to 1951 he was a pupil of composition of Frank Martin, a major Swiss-born composer; and in 1951 he continued the study of composition in Paris with Darius Milhaud and Olivier Messiaen. The influence all these teachers exerted on Stockhausen was negligible—Messiaen being the exception, since Messiaen was the one who first interested Stockhausen in using complicated rhythms and percussive sounds. Stockhausen at this time was writing more or less conventional music, though of course it was music modern in spirit and idiom, filled with discords, free rhythms, polytonal devices, and so forth.

While he was in Paris, Stockhausen was initiated to "Concrete Music." It was as if a new world had opened up for him. Convinced now that the future of music lay in electronics, Stockhausen studied physics and acoustics at the University of Bonn between 1952 and 1954. As far as composition went, he proceeded to forget most of what his teachers had taught him and started producing music in a serial technique which had also begun to fascinate him during his stay in Paris. His first serial composition was *Counterpoint (Kontrapunkte) No. 1,* for fourteen instruments in 1953, and *Piano Pieces* Nos. 1 through 9, completed between 1952 and 1954.

The writing of serial music, however, was but the beginning of his adventures in new music. We shall describe some of these adventures in later chapters. First, however, we must speak about his rendezvous with electronic music (or to borrow a term he invented for such creativity, "sound objects"), probably his greatest single contribution to the avant-garde movement.

One of Stockhausen's earliest compositions in the electronic field is still one of his best, *The Song of Youth (Gesang der Jüngling)* in 1956. Here the poignant voice of a boy soprano is heard in a musical setting of a text lifted from the Book of Daniel in the Bible; the voice is accompanied by nonmusical sounds produced on magnetic tapes. This combination of the sweet, piping voice of a boy singing within a comparatively formal style (even though the melodic idiom is highly modern), accompanied by noises in which all the formal patterns of music are discarded, produces a uniquely dramatic effect, new in our musical experience. *The Song of Youth* is, indeed, one of the most moving experiences that electronically produced music produced during its infancy.

If *The Song of Youth* represents the marriage of formal and electronic music, *Contacts (Kontakte)*, in 1960, on the other hand, was planned to be a struggle between instrumental parts recorded and distorted on magnetic tape (manipulated by the composer) and a piano and percussion instruments played by live musicians. To Raymond Ericson "the tape of electronic sounds, wholly prepared by the composer, suggests an aural landscape of considerable fascination." To Irving Kolodin, *Contact* provided evidence that "there is no doubt at all that electronics have given rise to a vast range of aural possibilities."

Stockhausen extended his electronic activities introducing potentiometers (which the *Random House Dictionary* defines as "a device for measuring electromotive force or potential difference by comparison with a known voltage"), an elektronium (another electronically manipulated instrument), and electronic filters, all manipulated by the composer. These are combined with live instruments—for example, the tam tam (a percussion instrument), viola and piano in *Procession (Prozession)* in 1967. A curious feature of this unusual work is that each of the five live musicians (two of whom have their instruments miked) improvise material from other earlier Stockhausen compositions!

Most of the electronic sounds produced today most fruitfully for serious creative purposes come from compositions like those by Stockhausen described above, which use magnetic tape with the sounds transmitted through loudspeakers. Largely through Stockhausen's influence, the importance of this revolutionary practice grew by leaps and bounds within a short period of time. Suddenly there sprang into being studios and laboratories for experimental work in this field. Within a decade there were over fifty such places in the United States alone, as, for example, those at Brandeis University in Waltham, Massachusetts, Princeton University, University of Illinois, Yale, University of Michigan, San Fernando Valley State College, Northridge (California), San Francisco Tape Music Center, Washington University, and St. Louis. Electronic studios were also founded in Toronto, Paris, Tokyo, Jerusalem, Milan, Warsaw, Buenos Aires, among other foreign cities.

The one in Milan—the Studio di Fonolgia Musicale at

the RAI Radio Station—was opened in 1954 by Luciano Berio (1923–   ). He is a brilliant young Italian musician who had been a dedicated serialist before he heard electronic music for the first time. He then came to regard Stockhausen as one of the world's greatest composers. Inspired by Stockhausen, Berio began working with electronic sounds in his Milan laboratory. One of his main contributions was to experiment with distortions of human voices, and one of his most exciting works is *Visages,* written in 1960, where a single voice utters a single word—the voice electronically distorted to pass the gamut of emotion from laughter to the most poignant sobs. The single word "parole" (Italian for "words") is used, and the voice is accompanied by electronic sounds. Still another such exciting use of distorted voice is found in Berio's *Homage to Joyce (Omaggio à Joyce),* in 1960, its text consisting of some forty lines from the second chapter of James Joyce's *Ulysses.* Here we first listen to the reading of the lines. After that the reading is distorted electronically with no other sound used but the voice. A critic for *High Fidelity Magazine* felt that Joyce's lines are here "transformed into a rich, elaborate and dramatic polyphony of pure sound." Since 1960, Berio has lived in America where he has pursued a highly productive career as composer and teacher.

The spread of electronic studios and laboratories is only one indication of the importance assigned to this altogether new way of sound-musical production. Another indication is that there now are a hundred or more composers, in many different parts of the world, whose creativity is committed *exclusively* to the electronic medium, while hundreds of others have used electronic means together with other avant-garde techniques. Some of the most novel and exciting music since 1950 has tapped electronic resources, so effectively that the significance of electronics in music can no longer be dismissed. Surely it is of no minor significance that in 1967 Dartmouth College, in Hanover, New Hampshire, instituted an annual competition for the best electronic composition submitted to it, the awards being made by the Dartmouth Arts Council. Nor is it less important to remark, for example, that in 1967 the composition selected for the Pulitzer Prize for music utilized electronic sounds: the String Quartet No. 3 by Leon Kirchner (1919–   ), introduced in New York on January 27, 1967. "The electronic element is used conservatively—discreet percussive accents and pitched 'woodwind' sounds mingle with the four strings," reported a critic for *High Fidelity Magazine*, "extending the textural range of the piece to almost orchestral proportions. At the work's conclusion the two stage loudspeakers take over completely, wresting the thematic material from the human players and turning it into a breath-taking contrapuntal display that mere live performers could never hope to equal. Totally routed, the strings can only answer this outburst with a final pianissimo chord, which sounds a knell of death."

Kirchner's prize-winning quartet combines actual instruments with electronic sounds. The 1969 Pulitzer Prize for music, however, went for the first time to a purely electronic composition which, since it was written for synthesizer, will be talked about in our next chapter.

Opera, too, has taken advantage of the fact that effects could be arrived at through electronics which no orthodox instruments or the human voice could duplicate. On May 31, 1959, Karl-Birger Blomdahl's electronic opera, *Aniara*, was introduced in Stockholm. It was so successful that it ran for fifty performances there, always to capacity houses. In 1960 this opera was heard and acclaimed in Germany and was recorded in its entirety; in 1967 it was chosen to represent Swedish opera at Expo '67 in Montreal, Canada.

"Aniara" is the name of a spaceship bound for Mars with passengers fleeing from earth, which has just been devastated by a nuclear holocaust. Thus *Aniara* is the first opera ever written about space travel; the first inspired by science fiction; and the first to use electronic sounds successfully. The libretto (by Erik Lindegren, adapted from a play by Harry Martinson) describes what happens, just before the arrival on Mars, when the ship encounters mechanical difficulties. It is incapable of reaching its destination, and must now drift forever aimlessly in space. It keeps traveling this way for twenty years during which the passengers pass from horror to despair to utter frustration. All sorts of cults and sects and superstitious beliefs spring up as the passengers try to find some meaning to their now aimless life. Then the people die off one by one until the last of them passes away. The opera ends with the voice and spirit of a "Blind Poetess" singing a hymn to Death in outer space, her song accompanied by weird electronic effects.

Though Blomdahl's score is compounded of many styles (jazz, folk music, atonality, the twelve-tone system, and so forth), it is in its use of electronic sounds that it achieves both its uniqueness and its dramatic force. Noises and sounds reproduced on doctored tapes are continually interpolated into the context of the score. The feeling of the supernatural is immediately projected into the opening prelude where electronic sounds and instrumental music are combined. Then over the whispering eerie electronic sounds we hear the chorus of emigrants chanting: "We come from earth, the only orb where life has found a land of milk and honey." The haunting impact on the listener is immediate—and it could not have been made with instruments and voices alone. As the opera begins with electronics so it ends with this medium to create a fantastic atmosphere. After the hymn of Death, we hear oscillating electronic sounds suggesting the utter desolation upon which the final curtain descends. Between the opening prelude and the closing sounds, electronics continually help to describe the desolate feeling of floating through immeasurable space, to underscore the terror that seizes the passengers as their doom becomes apparent to them, to point up their tensions, which keep ever mounting, and to portray the effect of the ultimate tragedy that befalls them.

Aniara was the first successful opera to use electronic devices for specific dramatic or atmospheric effects. Since then there have been many others—for example, Henk Badings' *Martin Korda, D. P.* in 1960, or Boris Blacher's *Incidents in a Crash Landing,* in 1966. The possibilities of electronics in opera, we now know, are limitless.

One of Stockhausen's convictions is that concerts as they are today given (with performer or performers on the stage facing the audience) are completely outmoded. This is the reason he started to work in an area he has designated as "new musical time space," but which other musicians have come to identify as "spatial" or "directional" music. This is music that converges on an audience from many different parts of the concert hall to produce a stereophonic effect. It should, however, be pointed out that experiments in this field had previously been done in America by Henry

Brant (1913–   ), a composer long fond of writing eccentric pieces of music as well as conventional works. On December 15, 1954, there took place in New York the première of Brant's *December*. Here the performers (singers as well as instrumentalists) were distributed all over the hall—some on stage, some in the box seats, some in the balconies. The effect of sounds converging at a central point, where the audience was seated, proved a real "shocker." It also gave sounds greater vividness of color and sonority, and unusual blendings.

December, however, did not attract much attention. But Stockhausen's *Groups (Gruppen),* in 1957, for three orchestras, most certainly did. Three different orchestras, each a self-sufficient entity with its own conductor, surround the audience by performing from three different places in the auditorium. As the composer himself explained: "They play . . . partially independently in different tempi; from time to time they meet in common rhythm; they call to each other and answer each other; for a whole period of time one hears only music from the left, or from the front, or from the right. The sound wanders from one orchestra to another."

Spatial, or directional, techniques were also used by Stockhausen in his electronic works *The Song of Youth* and *Contacts,* which we have mentioned before. The former was planned for a five-channel stereophonic system while in the latter, different groups are placed in different parts of the auditorium.

(Parenthetically, we might add that spatial music was used by both Badings in *Martin Korda, D.P.* and Blacher in *Incidents in a Crash Landing,* to endow their electronic sounds with a stereophonic effect. To give dramatic intensification to mob scenes, spatial music was employed by

Ginastera in *Don Rodrigo*—where the music of twelve horns converge on the audience from all possible directions —and in the highly publicized American opera, *The Visitation*, by Gunther Schuller in a lynching scene.)

Stockhausen also worked with noises, sometimes with exciting results. One of his most provocative works in this style is *Momente*, in 1962, where the sounds of thirteen musical instruments are combined with noises from monkey wrenches, cardboard tubes, plastic refrigerator containers filled with air-gun pellets, and other curious devices.

He has worked with other avant-garde techniques, too— with chance music, for example, and also with neo-dadaism. Since the high priest of both these idioms is John Cage, it might be wise for us to reserve our description of these Stockhausen compositions for our chapter on Cage.

Stockhausen has made several visits to the United States. On January 4, 1964, he appeared in a lecture-recital in New York when some of his more famous works were performed and when he discussed his aims in writing them. In 1966–1967 he returned to the United States to serve as visiting professor at the University of California in Berkeley. Thus America has had ample opportunity to become acquainted with this tall, slim, ascetic-looking man and to come to realize, through personal contacts with him, that he is no sensationalist, no trickster, no circus performer, not even a scientist seeking new truths in a laboratory. America has come to know that Stockhausen is a composer like any other, with the sole aim of expressing himself. "I am the product of many influences," Stockhausen has explained. "Naturally I draw upon them freely and sometimes unconsciously. My music makes sense to me. I can't ever understand why it poses problems for others."

| *They created music for computers and synthesizers.*

Yannis Xenakis

(1922–   )

Milton Babbitt

(1916–   )

Electronic music does not consist exclusively of musical sounds and noises produced on magnetic tape and amplified through loud-speakers. Electronic music has expanded far beyond the magnetic-tape era, since the time when Stockhausen first started his initial explorations in his Cologne radio laboratory.

There is, for example, the music that is produced by computers. Giant computers capable of performing highly complex mathematical problems with lightening rapidity have, of course, become essential to our industrial, governmental, and military complex—as well as to the advancement of outer-space adventures culminating with the landing on the moon. Feed into this giant mechanism a mass of data and it can in short order make harmony out of logistic chaos. Provide this machine with any number of variables and in no time at all it will assort them, discard what is irrelevant, and predict the behavior of substances. Stuff into it all known facts on any given subject or number of subjects and in split-second timing it can make up payrolls, give an exact account of inventories, operate machines automatically, foretell the flight of missles under every possible condition, and so forth. Computers, therefore, have become a monumental governing force in our daily life. They could not fail to touch the lives and work of composers as well.

What the computer does for the composer is to simplify the problem of creativity. All the composer has to do is to provide the computer with a variety of musical materials he plans to use for any given composition (various pitches, varieties of dynamics, durations of timbres, and so forth— but translated into computer language) and then the computer goes ahead and assorts all this material, rejects what it considers useless, and accepts and arranges the rest of the material into a logical sequence it considers serviceable. A fully written musical work emerges from the machine, which when deciphered from computer language back into musical notes, becomes a composition capable of being performed by traditional instruments, or sung in the traditional way. But it is important to remember that this composition, when it emerges from the computer, is as unfamiliar to the composer himself as it is to his public.

The first significant use of the computer to create music took place at the University of Illinois by Lejaren Hiller, director of its Experimental Music Studio. The University possessed a mammoth computer known as "Illiac" which Hiller used in an experiment to see if it could make music. In 1957, with materials fed into the machine, Hiller was responsible for the first piece of music to come out of a computer: the *Illiac Suite* which (once the computerized language had been translated into notes) was performed by a string quartet. The result was by no means music to shake the world. The composition *did* produce some interesting and unusual combinations of sounds, textures, and sequences which made any one movement of the suite an interesting aural experience but, regrettably, made the entire composition of four movements a bore. It has not been heard of since.

In 1959, Hiller, in collaboration with Leonard Isaacson, discussed computer music in print for the first time in the treatise *Experimental Music.* After that, collaborating with Robert Baker, Hiller produced a new work through the computer, *The Computer Cantata,* a giant advance over the *Illiac Suite. The Computer Cantata* was for live voice, live instrumental ensemble, an extended percussion section, and electronic sounds generated by the computer. A critic for *Hi-Fi Stereo,* Eric Salzman, considered the final result "an impressive web of sound." He went on to explain: "The vocal text is based on a kind of imaginary English invented by the computer out of the actual sounds of English. Fields of pitched sound and unpitched rhythmic percussion are played in big patches—something like color-field painting or certain aspects of abstract expressionism in which the big form is controlled but details fall out in random but perfectly consistent patterns."

One composer's name, above and beyond all others, is associated today with computer music. He is Yannis Xenakis

—architect, mathematician, philosopher, composer. Complicated though his music is (and his philosophic and mathematical theories on and explanations about his own music are more abstruse still), his influence has penetrated far and wide; some Polish musicologists have referred to our times as "the age of Xenakis."

Born in Athens, Greece, on May 29, 1922, he comes from a family of wealthy Rumanian businessmen. In Athens he studied engineering at the Polytechnic Institute, from which he was graduated. World War II changed the course of his life. The Nazis invaded Greece, and Xenakis joined the Resistance movement. Several times he was jailed and once, in combat, his face was permanently scarred and flattened. The Resistance movement in Greece was overcome. In 1947, Xenakis fled from his native land and settled in Paris. There he met and married a Greek girl who had also served in the Greek Resistance movement, who had also become an expatriate, and who later developed into a highly esteemed novelist. Xenakis became a French citizen in 1966.

In Paris, Xenakis interested himself in architecture, which he first studied with Le Corbusier, one of France's most highly renowned architects. In time Xenakis became Le Corbusier's assistant, helping him construct the Philips Pavilion at the Brussels Exposition in 1958. In 1960, Xenakis gave up architecture for good to devote himself to research in music. For a while, still plying the trade of architect, he had studied music seriously for the first time with such distinguished French musicians as Arthur Honegger and Darius Milhaud at the École Normale de Musique and with Olivier Messiaen at the Paris Conservatory.

His first major works used traditional instruments capable of producing untraditional sounds, pursuing a method and structure of his own devising. (He is one of the few avant-garde composers who did not begin their adventurous flights into music's future with either the twelve-tone or serial technique.) Being a mathematician, he related music to that science and evolved a creative process for which he invented the term "stochastic" (a word derived from the Greek "stochos" meaning "aim" or "conjecture"). What he was aiming at was compositions based on the laws of mathematical probability. Xenakis begins a composition with a simple bare sound. By the process of logical deduction he develops it according to the law of probabilities— in other words according to the probabilities of certain notes, rhythms, and sonorities recurring in a given work. Jan Maguire, a French journalist, described his method in the following way: "Instead of thinking in terms of harmony, as musicians have for many centuries, Xenakis thinks in terms of sound entities which possess the characteristics of pitch, intensity and duration as associated to each other by and within time." Xenakis' own description of his methods is typical of his poetic, philosophic, and technical language he always adopts whenever he talks about his music. He said, "There exist in a given space musical instruments and men; there is no cause or organization to produce sounds. But given a sufficiently long period of time it is probable that there will be a fortuitous generation of some sounds of certain lengths, certain colors, certain speeds, and so forth. . . . These are sound events . . . isolated sounds. They could be melodic figures, cellular structures, agglomerations whose characteristics are ruled by the laws of chance."

In 1953, he wrote *Metastis,* for orchestra, which begins with several measures on the note G sustained in the strings, while gliding glissandi in the rest of the orchestra and expanding dynamics help to achieve an overpowering climax. The overall effect is eerie, to say the least. Here, and in *Pithoprakata,* a composition for string orchestra that followed a year or so later, Xenakis explored the possibilities of simulating electronically produced sounds and sonorities with conventional instruments. The composer described this piece of music as a "dense cloud of sonorous material in movement." All kinds of sounds are produced by string instruments, by tapping the bodies of the instruments, by unusual use of bow and plucked strings, as well as by glissandi in the trombones. To the average listener, how the law of probability is here being followed is not easy to comprehend. Much easier is it for the average music lover, in listening to this explosive music with its completely unconventional sound textures within a formless structure, to interpret it in terms once outlined by the composer in one of his completely comprehensible statements: "In my music there is all the agony of my youth, of the Resistance, and the aesthetic problems they posed with the huge street demonstrations, or even more, the occasional mysterious deadly sounds of those cold nights of December '44 in Athens."

Xenakis soon became interested in electronic music. In 1958 he helped Edgard Varèse concoct the *Poème électronique* for the Philips Pavilion in Brussels (a work already touched upon in our chapter on Varèse). This was music produced on doctored tapes, a medium Xenakis continued to use in *Analogiques* in 1959, scored for nine strings and magnetic tape.

Then Xenakis involved himself with exploring the mathematical law of probabilities in music with the aid of a computer. The computer of his choice was the IBM dataprocessing system known as 7090, used commercially to plan the movements of oil fleets, to calculate the temperature of metals in furnaces, and to do market research. The machine was capable of doing 300,000 operations a second, and making 458,000 decisions a minute.

Jan Maguire explained that Xenakis "obtained figures to determine the length of sequence of sounds, their intensity and composition of the orchestra, as well as the moment of occurrence, pitch, speed, class of sound and instrument, and lengthened form of intensity." The machine makes its selections in codified machine language, which Xenakis then retranslates into musical notes. Thus one of his compositions was concocted, the machine having made its selection of all the musical materials Xenakis feeds into it in computer language. The machine then pours out a veritable shower of notes.

The first important work produced by Xenakis through the IBM Computer 7090 carries the unbelievable title of *St/10 = 1 − 080262 for Ten Instruments* (1962). "St" is an abbreviation for "stochastic." "10=1" refers to the fact that this is the composer's first composition for ten instruments. The number "080262" refers to the date when the computer concocted this composition: February 8, 1962.

Speaking of Xenakis' computer-made music, Jan Maguire adds: "Empirically the sound is often pleasant, although quite different from our musical diet. If the listener makes the mistake of looking for form or structure as he has always known it in music, he finds himself quite at sea. The structure of this music is not by any means readily apparent. It requires either a profound knowledge of mathematical laws or a profoundly relaxed and detached attitude on the part of the listener."

Xenakis has produced numerous works through the computer which are performed by traditional instruments. Most bear Greek titles. *Akrata,* for sixteen winds, has had numerous performances in Europe and America. *Achorripsis,* for twenty-one instruments, and *Eonta* for piano, four trumpets and six trombones, have also been widely heard and have been recorded. Such music, wrote Donald Henahan in *The New York Times,* "exerts a strong pull on the imagination, partly because we realize while listening that Xenakis' use of computers and physical laws have taken much of the actual composing out of his hands. It is as if we are granted a glimpse of the physical universe at work."

Xenakis has helped establish centers of electronic music where he has been pursuing his researches as well as his compositional endeavors. One of these centers is at the very place where computer music was born, the University of Illinois.

One of the American composers who has received direction and stimulus from Xenakis is Gerald Strang, composer of *Music for IBM 7090.* Whether or not Gordon Mumma, another American, has been similarly affected by Xenakis is not known, but he did use a computer (not the IBM 7090) in a highly provocative, original manner in *Conspiracy 8,* heard in New York on March 22, 1970. Onstage sat a teletype operator to inform the computer of what is occurring—a duet performed by Mumma on a "thirty-inch cross-cut saw" and David Behrman, playing on a viola. "The computer," explains a writer in *The New York*

Times, then flashes back "a suggestion that one of them should stop playing, that the flutist should join them in a trio or some such alternative. The players can then decide whether to obey or reject the suggestion. The human performers will have the same right to recommend how the piece will proceed. Assent or dissent will be an integral phase of the procedings."

Another important electronic device for the making of new music is the synthesizer. It differs from the computer in that the synthesizer does not make music with fed materials, but is an instrument on which the composer produces his own music directly, as if it were a piano or a pipe organ.

The first synthesizer was a giant machine, twenty feet long, seven feet high, with 1,500 tubes and innumerable devices for generating sounds. It was created by RCA at a cost of a quarter of a million dollars and was first demonstrated in 1955. A later development brought about the Mark II Synthesizer which *High Fidelity Magazine* has described as a device "completely programmed with punched paper tape, so that a complete series of events can be run through without interruption, while most smaller ones have to be 'played' with keyboards, knobs, slide switches and patch chords." Producing musical sounds through a synthesizer is basically a "filter operation, beginning with sawtooth waves, which contain all possible harmonics, and removing the unwanted ones, reinforcing the desired ones." One of the great advantages of the synthesizer over other electronically produced machines is that it allows the composer to monitor the sound he is producing *instantly,* thus permitting him to make whatever additions, revisions, and changes he finds necessary while the sounds themselves are being produced. Another important thing about the synthesizer is that it can emit any sound within man's experience, and an infinite range of sounds new to man.

An excellent description of how a composer works on a synthesizer was provided by Richard Kostelanetz in *The New York Times Magazine*. "On the face of the machine are switches that specify the following dimensions of musical sound—frequency (pitch), octave, volume, timbre, and envelope (degree of attack and decrease). When the composer assigns all the attributes of a note, the synthesizer immediately produces the sound. If the composer finds that the results suit his intentions he can affix it to the tape; if not, he can readjust the switches to make a new sound. . . . The composer can also piece one sound atop another (as is standard in tape doctoring), transform live sounds and even wholly original scales."

Through a grant from the Rockefeller Foundation, the Electronic Music Center was founded at Columbia and Princeton Universities in 1959—the first such affiliated with a university and entirely devoted to research in and composition of electronic music. It was there that there emerged the first notable composer for the synthesizer, the first to perform major experiments on the Mark II Electronic Sound Synthesizer and to write for it the first compositions heard in major concert auditoriums. That man is Milton Babbitt.

The son of an actuary, Milton Babbitt was born in Philadelphia on May 10, 1916. He received his early academic and musical education in Jackson, Mississippi. His musical training began with violin lessons when he was five and continued with lessons on the clarinet three years after that. He was still a boy when he began composing songs, creating words as well as music. But, as he has explained, his "early intellectual climate" was predominantly mathematical, since both his father and brother were mathematicians. Consequently, when Milton Babbitt entered college, he planned to concentrate on mathematics, while relegating music to a place of secondary importance. But, he confesses, "at the college I was appalled by the 'engineering' mathematics to which I was subjected and by the philistine attitudes towards logic and abstract mathematics which I encountered." Disenchanted with the kind of instruction he was getting, he began to show a rapidly mounting interest in music—especially the music of the twelve-tone masters. "I suddenly decided to exchange the degree of emphasis that I would place upon my two domains of interest, and to concern myself particularly with composition and theory."

At New York University he took courses in music theory and history; and when he left college he spent three years studying composition privately with Roger Sessions, an American composer with highly advanced (as well as complicated) tendencies in his own writing.

In 1938, Babbitt was appointed music instructor at Princeton University. There, four years later, he became a member of the first group receiving from that institution a graduate degree in music—a Master of Fine Arts.

The war involved Babbitt in military activities that were so highly secretive that they are still regarded as classified information. Upon leaving the army in 1943, he returned to Princeton, this time to join the department of mathematics. It was while thus involved that he first started evolving his musical theories in which he extended the twelve-tone system into serialism at virtually the same time that Pierre Boulez was doing the same thing in Paris. Babbitt wrote two compositions in the serial technique between 1946 and 1947. He even wrote a jazz work in the serial method: *All Set,* in 1957, which had been commissioned by the Brandeis Festival of the Creative Arts in Waltham, Massachusetts.

The year of 1958 was decisive for him, for it was then that he was asked by RCA to become acquainted with the Mark II Electronic Sound Synthesizer. Babbitt had, for twenty years, been thoroughly fascinated by the possibilities electronically produced sounds could offer a composer —and the Mark II Synthesizer represented to him the most advanced stage thus far achieved by electronics for the making of new music. For a while he worked on a different kind of synthesizer (the Olsen-Belar). Then when the Electronic Music Center of Columbia and Princeton Universities was founded in 1959 he concentrated on the Mark II Synthesizer.

His *Composition for Synthesizer,* in 1961, was not only his own first major work for this electronic instrument, but the first extended work produced by anybody for it. During the same year Babbitt also completed *Vision and Prayer,* for soprano, a setting of a poem by Dylan Thomas which became the first composition created for voice and synthesized accompaniment. It aroused such provocative arguments, pro and con, at the Congress of the International Musicological Ensemble that the synthesizer, aroused the curiosity and interest of numerous musicians who up to now had known little about it. Two more works for synthesizer were written by Babbitt in 1964: *Ensembles for Synthesizer,* introduced at the Ojai Festival in California,

and *Philomela,* for soprano, recorded soprano, and synthesized accompaniment. The latter had been commissioned
by the Ford Foundation and received a citation from the
New York Music Critics' Circle, the first work for synthesizer honored by this distinguished group. Meanwhile, in
1959, Babbitt became a member of the committee directing the Electronic Music Center at Columbia University
and Princeton and received an award from the National
Institute of Arts and Letters because he had shown "an
original and penetrating grasp of musical order that has
had a great influence on many younger composers." In
1960–1961 Babbitt received a Guggenheim Fellowship for
research in electronic music; in 1965 he was elected to the
National Institute of Arts and Letters; in 1966 he succeeded Roger Sessions as professor of music at Princeton;
and in 1970 Brandeis University, in Waltham, Massachusetts, conferred on him its Creative Arts Awards medal in
recognition of his long and distinguished record of achievement in electronic music.

In his compositions for synthesizer, Babbitt proved the
capacity of that electronic device to produce new and wider
rhythmic effects, ranges of sound frequency, and dynamic
possibilities heretofore unknown. A good deal of what can
come from a synthesizer cannot be duplicated or even ap-
proximated any other way: first, because no instruments
are capable of producing the vast variety of sounds a synthesizer can; second, because no existing performer has the
technique to produce on conventional instruments the
effects possible on a synthesizer. This is the reason why
Benjamin Boretz wrote: "Babbitt has demonstrated, with
almost revelatory impact, the enormous potential for significant musical development possible through a searching

reinterpretation of the fundamental principles of the perception and relation on which the continuity of Western musical tradition has been based."

The Pulitzer Prize committee recognized the importance of music produced through the Mark II Synthesizer when in 1970 it presented its award in music to Charles Wuorinen (1938–   ), an assistant professor of music at Columbia University since 1964. The winning composition was *Time's Encomium* in the twelve-tone system. This was the first time that the Pulitzer Prize ever went to a work that was exclusively electronic.

Wuorinen wrote *Time's Encomium* between January of 1968 and January of 1969 at the Columbia-Princeton Electronic Music Center on a commission from the Nonesuch Records, which released it in July of 1969. Thus this music was intended exclusively for a recording, and not for concert presentation. Wuorinen is the composer of over seventy-five works since producing his first symphony when he was twenty. He has been the recipient of many commissions and honors for works which require traditional instruments and are intended for traditional performances. But he has unbounded faith in the future of electronic music, and specifically for music produced on the Mark II Synthesizer.

It should not be assumed that the Mark II Electronic Sound Synthesizer is the only kind of synthesizer existing. There are others. Paul Ketoff, for example, devised a portable synthesizer, the Syn-Ket, whose importance rests in the fact that it can be transported to a concert stage. When, in 1968, John Eaton performed his own *Concert Piece for Syn-Ket and Symphony Orchestra,* "the audience quickly discovered," reported *Time*, "that there was nothing child-ish about the instrument. . . . Eaton's *Concert Piece* was able to achieve a dense, microtonal fabric of sound that would have made Charles Ives envious. Though the Syn-Ket started out with the familiar blips, snaps and bee swarming sounds usually associated with electronic music, it soon proved its special, if not necessarily pleasing, power with waves of organ-rich tones and descending spirals of patterned trills."

Then there is the device conceived by Robert Moog—the now extremely popular Moog Synthesizer—originally in-tended for commercial use exclusively. At first, its musical potential was highly primitive, since it could produce only a single tone at a time, thereby making it necessary for each voice of a composition to be played and recorded sepa-rately. At the urging of Walter Carlos, Moog has since de-veloped his synthesizer so that it can produce polyphonic compositions; at the same time, Moog introduced musical refinements and innovations enabling his synthesizer to create intonation, nuances, phrases, modulation, dynamics far more easily and far more authentically than had previ-ously been possible. This developed Moog Synthesizer now became a musical instrument, with an actual keyboard at-tached to the electronic machinery. (The Buchla Synthe-sizer dispenses with a keyboard, replacing it with a series of touch-sensitive plates.)

The Moog Synthesizer achieved national fame in 1969 when a Columbia recording, "Switched on Bach," became a best seller and in 1970 received a "Grammy" from the National Academy of Recording Arts and Sciences as the best classical album of the year. Here numerous Bach com-positions were performed on the Moog Synthesizer by Walter Carlos and Benjamin Folkman with a clarity of texture, an ability to re-create authentically and clearly tones producible on conventional instruments, while at the same time capable of approximating the sounds Bach must have had in mind when he wrote his music for the instruments of his own day rather than for those of our time. Bach here sounded as shining and new as a fresh-minted coin.

The greatest importance of the Moog Synthesizer is, of course, not in its ability to re-create the music of the past so well, but in its capabilities of arriving at new types of sounds and sonorities, since its tonal possibilities are virtually limitless. New jazz compositions written expressly for the Moog Synthesizer were heard at the Museum of Modern Art in New York on August 28, 1969—suddenly opening up new horizons for jazz music. On January 30, 1970, a new serious work, *The First Moog Quartet,* by Gershwon Kingsley (a scientist as well as a composer) was introduced by the composer and an ensemble. "Those unfamiliar with the capacities of Moog," commented Irving Kolodin, of the *Saturday Review,* "found the whoozes, wheezes, and plinks of sound unquestionably diverting. For those who have heard one Moog do extraordinary things and kind of expected four Moogs to do four times as many extraordinary things, the demonstration—at its earliest phases—was titillating. . . . The demonstration of capacities was certainly impressive."

The value of the Moog Synthesizer has spread far and wide. Of course, "Switched on Bach" was succeeded by a number of other well-selling recordings of music produced on that electronic instrument. In addition, the Moog Synthesizer made its classical concert debut in London in March of 1970 at the Royal Festival Hall. (By then there were at least four Moogs operating in Great Britain.) In Frankfurt, Germany, at about this same time, a ballet to music by Bach played on the Moog Synthesizer was the highlight of an evening of ballet at the Frankfort Opera House. And in America, a Moog Synthesizer was acquired by the Florida State University School of Music, which presented a concert of new works for that instrument by John Boda, professor at that University. The Moog Synthesizer was also used during a performance of Gian Carlo Menotti's opera, *Help, Help, the Globolinks!* by the Opera Guild of Tallahassee on April 23, 1970.

The Synthesizer, then—be it the Mark II, the Moog, or various other varieties—has already established its importance to the future of electronic music in general, and the music of tomorrow in particular.

VIII

*He developed music of chance
and neo-dadaism.*

John Cage

(1912–   )

There are very few fields in the avant-garde movement
in music that have not been fertilized by John Cage. As
we trace his career we shall comment upon his activities in
each of these areas. But two developments in our new
music which we have not yet described have involved John
Cage so deeply that, in spite of his work in other directions,
he is most often identified with them. One is "chance
music," for which the technical term is "aleatory music."
The other is music which penetrates the world of nonsense
and absurdity and for which long ago the word dadaism
had been coined; this is the reason why Cage's innovations
here are designated as "neodadaism," or "new" dadaism.

Chance, or aleatory, music, is that which is not produced
by careful planning and calculation the way symphonies,
concertos, or operas used to be; the composer no longer
works out the ideas he has previously clarified in his mind
over manuscript paper, works which always sound more or

less the same whenever they are performed. Chance music allows unpredictable elements to intrude, sometimes in the process of composition but most often during the performance. In creating music of chance a composer himself has no idea what his work will sound like until the chance method he has selected has been employed. During a performance of a piece of chance music, performers are often given discretionary powers to improvise their music while they are playing, so that in each performance the same composition sounds totally different.

Chance music is by no means a twentieth-century phenomenon. In the seventeenth and eighteenth centuries, one of the attractions of the concert was for a performer to improvise on the stage a piece of music on a given theme. Beethoven's first successes in Vienna as a young man came about through his unique powers at such spontaneous music-making. In those centuries, it was also the practice for virtuosos to improvise cadenzas to concertos; composers did not begin writing down their own cadenzas until the Romantic movement was in full swing. Chance methods were also basic to the jazz performances in New Orleans at the end of the nineteenth century when such greats as Joe "King" Oliver, Buddy Bolden, Bix Beiderbecke, and later on Louis Armstrong would, at the whim of a moment, and during the heat of a performance, suddenly engage in fanciful and thoroughly spontaneous improvisations inspired by, and greatly embellishing, some melodic or rhythmic thought.

Music produced by computers comes within the scope of chance music, too, since the composer has no idea how the machine will scramble up his materials, what it will select and reject, and precisely in what manner it will arrange the accepted materials into a musical composition.

Chance music today represents a reaction against serialism, since in serialism everything a composer puts down on paper is preordained by the rules of the game, his creativity thus being totally controlled. The other extreme is anarchy where a composer is bound by no rules, laws, formats, or formulas. The results of his creativity cannot be predicted beforehand. It is no coincidence—nor is it a paradox—that so many serial composers are also composers of chance music. Having constricted himself to a rigid, dictatorial method for so many compositions (even though this is a method the composer may believe in implicitly) he feels from time to time the necessity of veering to an opposite extreme by allowing himself the full freedom of letting chance, rather than technical laws, dictate the music he is to produce.

One way Cage has employed chance music is by writing out a piece of music for the piano on individual sheets of manuscript paper. The performer is advised to scatter the loose sheets haphazardly on the floor so that the manuscript becomes totally disarranged. The pianist then picks up one page after another at random and plays it until the last page on the floor has been picked up and performed. And then the composition is over. Since these loose sheets are scattered pell mell at each performance to create a new sequence, the composition sounds differently each time it is played—and its sound and structure have been determined purely by chance.

One of the processes Cage has employed in some of his works is "I Ching," meaning "Chinese Book of Changes." What this involves is the use of a pair of Chinese dice. Cage first worked out a table where the different numbers a throw of the dice is capable of producing is related to various elements in music. Cage throws out the dice and the number that comes up tells him what to put down on paper.

Many of Cage's larger works involving avant-garde idioms other than those of chance also take advantage of chance methods. In some works, (*Variations I* in 1958 and *Variations II* in 1961 to both of which reference will be made when we discuss neo-dadaism), the performers are permitted to decide for themselves what kinds of noises or sounds to produce. *Concert for Piano and Orchestra,* completed in 1958, which calls for extra-musical sounds and noises, is made up of eighty-four compositions. The performer is free to play the work in its entirety, or in part; to play any of the parts in whatever sequence he desires; and to keep on playing as long as he wishes by repeating various of the parts as often as he wants. In the *Theatre Piece* of 1965 (once again a composition that will be spoken about in our discussion of neodadaism) "parts are provided for one to eight performers (musicians, dancers, singers, et al.) to be used in whole or part, in any combination," the composer has explained. "This is a composition indeterminate of its performance. Time-brackets are given within which any action may be made. These actions are from a gamut of twenty nouns and/or verbs chosen by the performer. This gamut changes at given points, so that each part involves a performer in a maximum of fifty to one hundred different actions. Means are supplied for the answering of four questions, with regard to the activities within any one time bracket." For *Reunion,* in 1968, Cage requires electronics and a chess board to make his chance music. The chess board is electrified. Two people play a game, and the movements they create become magnified sounds by passing through an electronic filter.

Chance music, of course, is not a domain inhabited exclusively by Cage. One of Cage's most passionate and dedicated disciples is a New York composer, Morton Feldman (1926–   ), who maintains that his life as a musical creator really began in 1950 when first he came upon Cage's works. Feldman, like Cage, has thrown aside every concept and all the materials that the history of music has developed—serial music included. Feldman does not want one sound to have any relation to the next one in his compositions. He starts off by deciding how long a time is required to perform a piece of music he is planning. He then superimposes upon silence splashes of tones or sounds—silence being as important to the piece as the sounds—in the same way that avant-garde painters like Jackson Pollock or De Kooning indiscriminately threw blotches of paint upon an empty canvas. In fact, Feldman often quotes a phrase favored by De Kooning: "I work—other people call it art."

Chance plays an all-important role in Feldman's work. Here is how Theodore Strongin of *The New York Times* described Feldman's *Vertical Thoughts,* which was performed in New York in 1965. "Four of the five movements left performers free to decide when they should enter. They were instructed to begin as the sound of the preceding instrument faded. There were measured areas of silence and of simultaneous sounds, decided upon in advance by the composer. But, mostly, the performer listened and chose his own crucial moment to begin playing." Another Feldman work heard at this same concert was *Straits of*

Magellan, which was described in the program as a "graph piece." The pitch of the notes were not specified, but the duration of the notes and the number of sounds to get played were indicated to last a certain length of time. Explaining his chance methods, Feldman has said: "Unlike improvisation, which relies solely on memory in selecting the most empirical and sophisticated examples of a style, or styles, the purpose of the graph is to erase memory, to erase virtuosity—to do away with everything but a direction action in terms of the sound itself." Feldman's earliest experiments with "graph music"—a term he prefers to "chance"—came between 1950 and 1951 with *Projection No. 1,* for solo cello, and two orchestral works, *Intersection No. 1* and *Marginal Intersection.* In the first of these, as Feldman has written, "registers (high, middle and low), time values, and dynamics (very low throughout) were designated" while "actual pitches within the given registers were freely chosen by the performer." In the latter two works "not only actual pitches within the registers, but also dynamics and entrances within the given time structure were freely chosen by the performer."

Frequent use of chance methods has also been made by Karlheinz Stockhausen, whose electronic compositions have already been covered. In 1956, Stockhausen completed *Tempo (Zeitmesse)* where the performers can change the tempo any way they desire. This piece is scored for flute, oboe, English horn, clarinet, and bassoon. Sometimes one of the instruments is instructed to play as fast or as slowly as humanly possible, while other instruments can improvise their own tempo accordingly. Individual performers are allowed to interpolate improvised cadenzas, though the materials he must use are carefully set down by the composer. (When a composer furnishes the materials—the basic pitches, rhythms, dynamics, and so forth to be used during the performance for improvisation—the method has come to be called "controlled chance.")

Another chance piece by Stockhausen is *Piano Piece XI (Klavierstuck XI)*, written in 1956. This is made up of nineteen fragments. The pianist can not only play these fragments in whatever sequence he desires, but is free to use any one of six designated tempo markings, dynamic markings, and types of touch selected by the composer. When a fragment has been repeated three times the composition is over.

In Stockhausen's *Cycle (Zyklus)* for percussion instruments, in 1961, chance is again "controlled." Though this piece requires just one performer, he is required to play a wide variety of percussion instruments all grouped in a circle. The percussionist goes from one instrument to another until the circle has been rounded. He can begin on any measure in the score—even in the middle of the work —and continue on until he comes back to the measure with which he had started. At this point the performance has been completed.

In 1961, Pierre Boulez wrote a five-section piano sonata (his third) where once again the pianist can play the parts in any sequence, or is free to omit one or more sequences. In *Improvisations on Mallarmé*, written some three years earlier, Boulez allows the singer to improvise at will, though only with materials provided for this purpose ("controlled chance" once again). The rest of the work, for orchestra, is in strict serial technique—written-down music which the instrumentalists must play as designated.

Lukas Foss, the brilliant American conductor and composer, and now one of the staunchest advocates of avant-garde music, used to be a composer with Romantic tendencies and traditional techniques and structures. In some of his compositions in which the text is based on the Bible, he combined his Romanticism with the contrapuntal methods of the seventeenth century. But in the latter part of the 1950s, Foss turned his back to the past and faced the future boldly by exploring as fully as he could the possibilities of chance as a creative process. "It all began modestly as a means of helping my students," Foss has explained, "but suddenly a door opened for me and I saw a vast new territory to explore."

In 1957 Foss founded the Improvisation Chamber Ensemble comprising four members. Their performances (all over the United States) consisted of works improvised during the actual concert. For this group Foss concocted the *Concerto for Improvising Solo Instruments and Orchestra* in 1960, for which he devised a complicated chart on which were marked off various thematic ideas, rhythmic patterns, entrances and exits of each of the four solo instruments, and other compositional elements. The soloists were allowed to use this material during the concert any way their hearts dictated, developing Foss's germinal ideas into fully developed musical works.

In one of his most important works, Foss worked out a method of combining chance and written-down music. This is the *Time Cycle,* four songs for soprano and four instrumentalists (piano, clarinet, cello, and percussion) and orchestra, written in 1960 to texts by W. H. Auden, A. E. Housman, Kafka, and Nietzsche. The singers deliver the written-down music accompanied by the orchestra, while the four instrumentalists remain silent. When the song is finished, the four instrumentalists take over to improvise a kind of tonal commentary on the song just heard, this time with the singer and orchestra remaining silent. When *Time Cycle* received its world première in New York in 1960 with Leonard Bernstein conducting the New York Philharmonic, Bernstein regarded this so important a composition that when he completed his performance he repeated it a second time so that the audience might become better acquainted with it. *Time Cycle* received the New York Music Critics' Circle Award in 1961 as the most important new work of the season.

Foss's explanation of why chance music so fascinated him provides us with the reason why Cage has pursued this method so passionately, and with so much dedication. Foss explained that it was highly desirable to have a composition sound differently at each performance for the following reasons: "For the pleasure of surprise—not so much the audience's, who may hear the piece but once, but the performer's. He will experience surprise at every performance (a) because the detail is always different, (b) because though always different, the music remains somehow curiously the same."

If there is to many people a suggestion of the ridiculous in the process of producing music by chance then, surely, these same people must regard Cage's neodadaistic works as outright absurdity.

Cage did not invent dadaism; he revived it. Dadaism represents a glorification of nonsense—be it in poety, art, literature, or music. Escape from reality into nonsense usually comes at a time when society is afflicted by futility and disenchantment. Thus dadaism first came into existence during World War I to become an avenue of escape for all those who were disgusted with the way lives and property were destroyed, and who were war weary.

We know exactly when dadaism was born: on February 8, 1916, at 6 o'clock in the evening. We also know where: at the Terrace Café in Zurich, Switzerland. The parent of dadaism was Tristan Tzara. Tzara coined the term at that place to describe a new art—the art of absurdity—in order (as his friends put it so indelicately) "to spit in the eye of the world." They made plans to devote an entire evening to dadaistic art at the Cabaret Voltaire in Zurich the following February 26. Participating in this event were such now world-famous representatives of art and culture (most of whom were still unknown in 1916) as Picasso, Apollinaire, Modigliani, Kandinsky, and Marinetti. Nonsensical canvases, songs and poems and speeches that were sheer gibberish, and sketches made up of the most ridiculous situations were the features. Numerous other similar soirées followed in Zurich. It was not long before some serious-minded composers became part of this movement.

In 1919, Darius Milhaud of France composed the music for *The Nothing Doing Bar (Le Boeuf sur le toit)*, the scenario by Jean Cocteau being a dadaistic pantomime. The characters in this strange bar include a Negro dwarf, a Negro boxer puffing on a huge cigar, a woman with paper hair, a fashionable woman who flings the dwarf over her shoulder, and a policeman who is decapitated when a huge revolving fan falls on him. When the dwarf refuses to pay his bar bill, the bartender quietly removes his own head and places it on the body of the policeman who then suddenly comes to life again. The policeman shows the dwarf his bill, which is two feet long. For all these queer goings on and eccentric characters, Milhaud created a light, jaunty score made up of South American popular music, including tangos and sambas.

In this dadaistic movement we also find an English poet, Edith Sitwell (a member of a famous literary family). She wrote a set of nonsense verses, *Façade,* in order "to obtain a new kind of gaiety," as she put it. Her poems made no sense, the humor arousing from the sounds produced by the words ("Daisy and Lily, Lazy and Silly, Walk by the shore of the wan grassy sea, Talking once more neath a swan bosomed tree"; or, "Lily O'Grady, Silly and Shady, Longing to be a Lazy Lady"). A young English composer recently come from Oxford and a close friend of the Sitwells—the now world-famous Sir William Walton—provided the music for this score, holding his tongue square in his cheek. His music is made up of popular tunes, satirical melodies, parodies of the music of other composers, comic musical effects, caricature, and so forth. On June 12, 1923, *Façade* was heard for the first time anywhere, in London. The stage curtain had on it a painted face whose mouth was shaped like a tremendous megaphone. Behind the curtain, Edith Sitwell recited her poems in sing song style, her voice emerging from the large, distorted mouth on the curtain. Seven instrumentalists provided the accompaniment—hidden from view. This performance caused some laughter, some shock, some outrage. But *Façade* has not been forgotten. It has survived in the orchestral repertory through two suites for large orchestra which the composer had adapted from his score. Most usually this music is heard without the words, and always proves a source of the most delightful musical entertainment. Sometimes, however, Edith Sitwell's words are also used, as happened in a fine recording released by Columbia.

For the most part, dadaism passed from public interest in the late 1920s. I say "for the most part" because it is possible to consider Virgil Thomson's opera *Four Saints in Three Acts* (1934) dadaism, since the text by Gertrude Stein is totally undecipherable and the dialogue frequently has no meaning whatsoever. (To contribute further nonsense, this opera is in reality in four acts and not in three, and there are more than four saints in the cast.) Boris Blacher's opera *Abstract Opera No. 1 (Abstrakte Oper No. 1)*—which caused a scandal when it was staged for the first time in Mannheim in 1953—may also be looked upon as dadaism. For here the text is without plot, the dialogue once again makes very little sense, and frequently considerable use is made of meaningless sounds. Notwithstanding the emergence of one or two such works, dadaism lost its vogue until John Cage revived it in the 1960s. And once again the presence of dadaism was an expression of the cynicism and frustrations harassing a troubled era, providing a flight from disagreeable realities.

Three works by Cage, all introduced in 1965, are characteristic of his neodadaistic tendencies. *Variations V* requires the services of dancers, electronic equipment, and a screen on which distorted images from television and motion-picture clips are flashed. The main male dancer, wearing red pants and a gray shirt, rides a bicycle through a mass of electronic transmitters which capture the sounds of the bicycle movements and transmit them through loudspeakers scattered throughout the auditorium.

In *Theatre Piece* we see a man hanging upside down, wrapped in a black plastic cocoon. During the proceedings,

Charlotte Moorman (a cellist who has made a specialty of neodadaism) performs a composition by Cage while the composer puts into and removes from her mouth a cigar. A tiny Japanese gentleman waves silken banners hung atop huge bamboo poles. Balloons are punctured; buzzers are sounded; all kinds of electronic noises are projected. This presentation even requires activity *outside* the auditorium: a tiny oil drum is rolled down the stairs.

Cage's influence led numerous other composers to invade the strange, irrational world of neodadaism. Mauricio Klagel, an Argentine, wrote *Mimetics* where, if the performer so desires, he can play any composition he wishes by any other composer in counterpoint to one of the sections of Klagel's work. Neodadaism is injected through the bouncing of a rubber ball by one of the instrumentalists and a loud conversation by two other musicians during the performance.

Gÿorgy Ligeti's *Adventures* is neodadaistic in the way in which he uses everyday vocal sounds as part of his scoring. The music is continually punctuated by "shouts, gulps, gasps, swoops, ahems, moans, laughs, groans," as Eric Salzman wrote in *Stereo Review.* "The effect is at first comic, then dramatic. . . . The instruments pick up where the voices leave off and both instrumental and vocal interjections take place in a curiously empty universe—as if it were more difficult and even more necessary than ever to make art and artistic expression in the void."

Nam Jun Paik, a Korean now residing in America, wrote *Action Music* which was on the program of the festival of avant-garde music held in New York in 1965. Here is what happened, according to a report by Herbert Klein in *The New York Times:* "The opening consisted of the composer doing an action painting with black paint applied by both hands and hair entitled *Homage to Cage*. After that, one of the upright pianos was smashed, eggs were broken, and roars came from loud-speakers through electronic means. This was followed by nails being driven into one of the pianos, with Mr. Paik cutting his hair, with bedecking several men and women with strips of shaving cream, with cutting off the tie and shirt of one man with a scissors. The high point of the performance came when Charlotte Moorman played the cello. She played *Variations on a Theme by Saint-Saëns*, wearing as her dress a costume consisting solely of a cellophane sheath. While she played, the composer held the end pin of the cello in his teeth. Midway in the performance of Saint-Saëns' *The Swan*, Miss Moorman climbed a six-foot ladder and jumped into an oil drum filled with water. Then she climbed out, her cellophane sheath clinging to her body, to complete the playing of *The Swan*."

Chance music and neodadaism represent just a fraction of Cage's often curious and outlandish and sometimes rewarding experiments. He had worked intensively with musical noises and with electronics, for example. Time and again—in one composition after another—he has dared to rush in where fools would fear to tread.

He was born to highly cultured parents in Los Angeles on September 5, 1912. His father was a successful inventor; his mother, an editor on the *Los Angeles Times*. John received musical training early with local piano teachers, revealing talent from the very beginning. Nevertheless, he seemed incapable of relating himself completely to the music he was required to play (the Classical and Romantic literature). He did not abandon his music study, however.

While attending Pomona College, in Claremont, California, from 1928 to 1930, he studied the piano with Fannie Charles Dillon. And after leaving college, he continued his music study in Paris with Lazare Lévy.

Despite his intensive preoccupation with the piano, he knew that his future in music would lay in composition rather than performance. He embarked upon an intensive study of theory and composition with such advanced modernists as Arnold Schoenberg and Edgard Varèse, among others. It was first now that he found himself reacting strongly—both emotionally and intellectually—to music as never before. His full awakening in music took place when he was introduced to the twelve-tone system. This, for him, offered a shining new world which he was restless to explore. He was particularly fascinated by Anton Webern, and the way in which Webern used fragments and individual tones instead of fully developed themes, and in the effective way Webern punctuated his music with silences. Excited by a technique which so suited his own personality and thinking, Cage completed several works between 1933 and 1939 using the twelve-tone technique rigidly; the most important of these compositions was a five-movement suite for the piano, *Metamorphosis,* in 1938.

His enthusiasm for the twelve-tone system was nurtured and developed during his studies with Schoenberg and other twelve-tonalists. Edgard Varèse introduced Cage to his own world of extra-musical sounds and noises. Cage started working with music for percussion instruments in which the element of rhythm was all-important. He regarded this experiment as an extension of his twelve-tone writing, saying: "The theory of percussion is very much akin to atonal music. No sound any more important than any other comes out of atonal music into organized sound." In 1936, while serving as a member of the music faculty at the Cornish School in Seattle, Washington, Cage gave concerts of percussion music. During this period he wrote several works exclusively for percussion, among them the *Second Construction* and the *Third Construction,* both for percussion sextet, between 1939 and 1941. With each successive *Construction* he became increasingly daring and original. In the *Second Construction* he used metal and skin percussion instruments and a string piano capable of creating sirenlike sounds when a cylinder on the strings was made to slide whenever a trill was played on the keyboard. In his *Third Construction* he used tin cans, cowbells, a lion's roar, a cricket caller, a conch shell, together with more or less conventional percussions. For these noises Cage coined the phrase "rhythmed sounds."

Like his teacher Varèse, Cage had to fly on his own wings. And so, during this period, he tried to produce new sounds from the piano by a process he called "preparing." This meant stuffing all kinds of materials between the strings on the soundboard: bolts, screws, nuts, wood, felt, spoons, clothespins, boxes. Thus new sonorities and sound qualities are brought into existence, and the old concepts of precise pitch and formal scales are discarded. To Cage, the "prepared piano" was like a one-instrument percussion ensemble for a single performer.

Cage's first piece for a "prepared piano" was *Bacchanale,* in 1938, written as background music for a short one-woman dance routine. He needed percussion sounds for the effects he was then seeking, and he had only a piano to work with—so he adapted the piano to serve his aesthetic aims. A decade later, between 1946 and 1948, Cage com-

pleted his most significant music for "prepared piano"—
Sonatas and Interludes. This is a seventy-minute work
where "preparing" the piano is so complex an operation
that several hours are needed for this purpose. Some critics
have called Cage's music for the "prepared piano" as "children's games for adult ears," and the instrument itself as
"an old piano that should be thrown away." But others
were far more favorable in their reactions—the composer-
critic Lou Harrison, for example, who wrote: "The tension
and strength that a few quiet tones convey . . . are a sign
of a completely new and authentic creative power." And
another distinguished composer-critic, Virgil Thomson,
wrote that Cage's compositions for the "prepared piano"
represented "not only the most advanced methods now in
use anywhere but original expression of the highest poetic
quality."

"Rhythmed sound" assumed increasing significance in
Cage's work. In 1940 came *Living Room,* where sounds
normally encountered at home were reproduced, such as
banging of doors, closing of windows, moving about of
furniture. These noises were recreated by percussion instruments, but this work also enlists a speech quartet.
Imaginery Landscape No. 1, in 1942, is scored for tin cans,
buzzers, water gong, a metal wastebasket, a lion's roar, and
an amplified coil of wire. For *Imaginery Landscape No. 2,*
in 1942, Cage required electronic and mechanical devices,
including audio-frequency oscillators, a variable speed
turntable for the playing of frequency recordings, gener-
ator whines, and a buzzer. *Landscape No. 4,* in 1951, used
twelve radios operated by twenty-four players, two opera-
tors for each radio. Sounds of various radio programs, together with squeals and static, were all combined into a

new kind of cacophony. One year later Cage produced *Water Music* for radio (operated by a pianist), a whistle, water containers, and a deck of playing cards. The radio produced static; the water containers contributed the sounds of water being poured from a full container into an empty one, this process being regulated by a stop watch; the deck of cards introduced a novel effect by being riffled. *Williams Mix,* in 1952, captured the sounds of the city streets, amplified on magnetic tape. Noises appear in his 1958 *Concerto for Piano and Orchestra* in which the pianist is required to creep under the instrument and thump the wood on the underside, and after that to manipulate electronic devices. In *Fontana Mix,* in 1958, the following sounds are introduced in amplification on magnetic tape: cigarette ashes dropping into ashtrays; scraping wires and microphones on the strings of a piano keyboard; putting on and taking off eyeglasses; the sounds of swallowing, cigarette-smoking, grunting, coughing (microphones being attached to the throats of several of the performers); the scraping of microphones over glass. "This use of everyday music," Cage explains, "makes me aware of the world around me. Now I go to a cocktail party, I don't hear noise, I hear music."

If Cage has been an apostle of noises, he has also made a fetish of silences. What is probably the ultimate in the use of silences comes in *Four Minutes Thirty-Three Seconds,* which Cage "wrote" for the piano in 1952. All the performer is required to do is to sit at the keyboard and play nothing for four minutes and thirty-three seconds! It is not difficult to make a mockery of this quixotic exercise. The brilliant Hollywood composer for the screen and winner of numerous "Oscars"—John Green—did it in his own inimitable way. Required to lecture on avant-garde music, Green announced he would now present Cage's *Four Minutes Thirty-Three Seconds* reproduced on tape. Naturally, no sounds emerged. After a minute and a half Green shut off the tape machine and commented: "You will notice that I played only one and a half minutes of this strange composition, but that is because I have done some very careful editing."

One can dismiss *Four Minutes Thirty-Three Seconds* as a "stunt"—which it is. A good many musicologists, musicians, and musical societies, however, do not regard Cage's other excursions beyond the boundaries of musical reason lightly. For example, the Guggenheim Foundation awarded him a fellowship in 1949 for "creative work" in his various fields of musical endeavors. The National Academy of Arts and Letters soon thereafter gave him an award for extending the "boundaries of music." In 1963 Cage came to the Zagreb Music Biennale in Jugoslavia as the representative from America to lecture on his aims and ideas and to direct a concert of his own music—"unquestionably the most talked-about figure at the Biennale," reported Gunther Schuller. At the University of Cincinnati he was made composer-in-residence in 1966 and 1967. The National Institute of Arts and Letters elected him a member. One of Poland's foremost living composers, Witold Lutoslawski, (after having achieved international fame for writing splendid music in comparatively traditional styles) became so impressed with Cage's work heard at the Darmstadt Festival in Germany in 1961, that the experience "provided a spark that ignited a powder keg in me. I was a mature composer with many things to express but in fifteen minutes I had an insight into new possibilities open to me by incorporating into my music Cage's ideas." Ezra Laderman, in a feature article in *The New York Times Magazine* on September 11, 1966, said: "We do not have a single composer with a European reputation, with the exception of George Gershwin and John Cage," and then went on to comment that Cage "is the first American composer, excepting Gershwin, truly to change the thinking of a tremendous number of European composers from Poland to Greece. The younger composers, the fledgling musicians abroad, flock to him."

Harry Partch

(1901–   )

In preceding chapters we have seen that there are more ways than one to make a permanent break with the past in music and progress toward a brave new world.

Harry Partch has had a way all his own to create a new music. Unlike other avant-garde pioneers with new revolutionary methods and techniques he has no imitators—just as he himself was no imitator. Partch never adopted the twelve-tone technique or serialism, both of which he regarded as a strait jacket for his own wild, uninhibited creativity. He renounced the world of electronics (even though on one or two occasions he did try to interpolate prerecorded taped sounds into his compositions). "Electronic music," he said, "is too impersonal. Music has validity for me only as human expression. It must be corporeal. Man, not machine, is the ultimate instrument." Partch finds no value in "chance music" since "for me everything must make its own kind of logic, everything must be pre-determined, systematically conceived."

Yet he, too, felt with unwavering conviction that the materials provided by music's past were obsolete. He, too, heard strange, new, exotic sounds which nobody else was producing and which demanded from him to be heard. And so to bring those sounds to life he had to invent his own scale, his own musical instruments, his own notation, his own musical aesthetics.

There are more ways than one in which Partch reminds us of Charles Ives—above and beyond the superficial facts that he, too, has a straggly beard, a lined and somewhat gaunt face, eyes that reveal the strength and determination of a prophet, and a partiality for rough, unkempt clothes. He, too, has a weakness for whimsy; he, too, has remained oblivious to the demands of the musical marketplace, pre-ferring to travel along his own lonely road, ignored by most of the music world. But where Ives wrote for himself alone and never tried to get either performances or com-mercial publications, Partch has for years tried to bring his message and his music to the attention of the world. He recorded his music under his own label (Gate V) and with one or two other minor recording studios. He has written about his highly personal methods and ideas in out-of-the-way intellectual journals as well as in a book published in 1949, *Genesis of a Music*. Notwithstanding such efforts, Partch remained little known in America, outside a small sphere in the West where he makes his home and where a handful of admirers have for some time made him into something of a cult. Strange to say, he also found believers among a number of European musicologists and musicians.

But to most of America his name was not known—let alone his theories, innovations, and music.

He originated his own musical language first by concocting a new scale. (Others who have preceded him in this included Alexander Tcherepnin, who conceived a nine-tone scale, and Henk Badings, who evolved a new scale by alternating major and minor modes.) With Partch the conventional octave was divided into forty-three intervals, thereby necessitating the use of intervals smaller than the half tones found in our traditional scales. Music with intervals smaller than the half tone is known as "microtonal." Microtonal music, once again, is nothing new with Partch. Ives had experimented with it a half century earlier; Ernest Bloch, an American composer of Swiss origin, achieved quarter-tone effects in his First Piano Quintet, and Béla Bartók, Hungary's foremost twentieth-century composer, used quarter-tone ornamentation in his String Quartet No. 6. In Czechoslovakia, Alois Haba worked extensively with quarter tones, writing many microtonal works including an opera, *The Mother*, and inventing instruments capable of performing quarter-tone music. In the 1920s and early 1930s an American pianist-composer, Hans Barth, perfected a quarter-tone piano and wrote for it various compositions, among them a concerto accompanied by a string orchestra playing instruments tuned in quarter tones. (This concerto was heard at a concert of the Philadelphia Orchestra conducted by Leopold Stokowski on March 28, 1930.) But Partch carried the technique of microtonal music far beyond these earlier efforts. The forty-three interval scale he uses is something he himself has invented.

For his compositions, Partch requires the use of unorthodox instruments, most of them of his own making: a viola with an elongated neck which is played like a cello; a seventy-two string kithara which has the shape of an ancient lyre; a thirty-six wood-block diamond marimba with bamboo resonators; a bass marimba with eleven spruce blocks over redwood resonators; "cloud-chamber bowls" built from sawed-off glass vats; six- to ten-string guitars; something called "bloboys" (and sometimes "Spoils of War") made of artillery casings; bellows; a 1912 auto horn; a device called a "whang gun," and something else he named the "boos," the latter consisting of giant-size bamboos and marimba-like reeds; a "chormelodeon," which is really an altered pipe-organ; and various curious odds and ends to which he gave the strange names of "eucal blossom," "gourd tree and cone gongs," "mazda marimba," (the last comprising rows of light bulbs), "cry-chords," "zymo-xyls," and so forth. Some of his instruments—and a good deal of his musical thinking—reveal the influence upon him of ancient Greece, the Orient, Yaqui Indians, Hebrew and Christian chants, the Polynesian islands and other esoteric places, peoples, and cultures.

He finds no value in "pure" music as such—the kind of formal music-making heard in today's concert halls. For Partch, music should be part magic, part ritual. It must be seen as well as heard. It must be a kind of ceremony in the same way that the Japanese "Noh" plays or the ancient Greek dramas were ceremonies. Words, dance movements, miming, even slapstick must all come within music's province. Music, Partch insists, must have no relation to present-day society. What Partch tries to do is to return to ancient cultures where music was more instinctive than calculated. Harry Partch (like Ives before him) is a one-of-a-kind composer, *sui generis*. Peter Yates rightly referred to him as "one of those inspired, stubborn radicals of creative thought who never exactly fits anywhere."

"I am a hobo," is the way Partch describes his picaresque life, which has truly been as unconventional as his music, filled with a variety of unusual experiences in many different places.

He was born in Oakland, California, on June 24, 1901. He was the son of parents who had been missionaries in China. Partch's boyhood was spent not in California (where he now makes his home) but in Arizona, near the Mexican border, since his father had found a post there as immigration officer. Partch's mother, an amateur organist, gave Harry some music lessons, the only formal instruction he was ever to receive. Self-taught, he soon began playing the reed organ, mandolin, cornet, violin, and harmonica when he was about six years old. At fourteen came his first compositions (all of them conventional in style). In Albuquerque he supported himself by playing the piano and mechanical organ in movie theaters: movies were then silent and required continual live musical background. Later on he took on various other jobs, such as that of a migrant fruit-picker, proofreader for a newspaper, and schoolteacher. All this while he kept on writing music. By the time he was twenty-two he had completed a string quartet, a tone poem for orchestra, a piano concerto, and some fifty songs. When he was twenty-eight he burned all of this music in a potbellied stove.

Under a Carnegie grant he was able to spend several years in London concentrating on the study of the history of intonation at the British Museum. Back in the United States, which was then in the depths of an economic depression since this was the period of the early 1930s, he was forced to ride the rails in order to come intimately into contact with American life, its geography, backgrounds, people, and cultural influences. He spent about eight years as a "hobo." All this time he was collecting the material he would use in his compositions while clarifying and crystallizing new theories and concepts about the directions he should follow as a composer.

He was employed as lumberjack in the West when the news reached him that he had been awarded a Guggenheim Fellowship to do experimental work on the new instruments he required for the performance of the revolutionary type of music he was now beginning to conceive. This was in 1943. Since the Fellowship was renewed for a second year, he could now devote himself to manufacturing his own instruments; at the same time he worked upon the first compositions in which his striking individuality came strongly to the fore.

His experiences while wandering as a hobo around the United States and picking up all types of personal adventures while engaging in menial occupations—all this proved a source from which Partch drew the stimulation for his first major works, in 1943. He called it *U.S. Highball: A Musical Account of a Transcontinental Hobo Trip,* scoring it for chorus and instruments. In this work he aimed to point up, as he explained, "the disintegration of urban civilization and the pathos of the outcast's search for the spring of life." The text (narrated or chanted by a hobo named "Mac") is made up of the names of railway stations, the slogans on billboard advertisements, and Partch's own random thoughts as he traveled about. The background music re-creates railroad noises, while fragments of melodies of hillbilly tunes and popular songs are freely interpolated.

It was in the 1950s that his forty-three tone scale and his wide assortment of esoteric instruments came into full play. During this period he wrote *Barstow* (its subtitle explains that it is based on "eight hitchhiker inscriptions from a highway railing at Barstow, California). Partch facetiously refers to this composition as his "hobo concerto." Other compositions of this period include *Daphne of the Dunes,* which had originated as the soundtrack for a motion picture, *Wind Song.* When it was heard in New York at the Juilliard School of Music in 1959 (three years following its world première at the University of Illinois), Jay Harrison wrote in review: "Mr. Partch's instruments give off a rainbow luminosity. . . . The score itself is mainly incantational, an effect close to hypnosis being Mr. Partch's ultimate world. . . . Surprisingly, in all works, all comes off with remarkable vibrancy. . . . In the final analysis, it makes an authentic communication."

Bewitched, one of Partch's most exotic works, was derived from the Japanese Kabuki theater. A group of lost clown-musicians serve as principal characters to destroy the spurious output of twentieth-century mechanization and intellectualism. "They are primitive," explains Partch, "in their unspoken acceptance of magic as real, unconsciously reclaiming an all-but-lost value for the exploitation of their perception." Episodes in *Bewitched* provide the audience with a clue to the composer's programmatic intentions through their respective titles, such as "A Soul Tortured by Contemporary Music Finds a Humanizing Alchemy," or "The Cognoscenti are Plunged into a Demonic Descent with Cocktails," or "Visions Fill the Eyes of the Defeated Baseball Team in the Shower Room."

Though both *Daphne of the Dunes* and *Bewitched* were given in New York—the first in 1944, the latter in 1959—Partch did not come into his own as a composer in that city until September 8, 1968, with a concert of his works at the Whitney Museum of American Art (which at that time was offering an exhibit of Partch's instruments). This concert was given for specially invited guests; but two nights later it was open to the general public, and was recorded by Columbia. The program was representative of Partch's adventures as composer, with specimens of his work influenced either by ancient cultures or by modern Americana. The performance opened with two studies on ancient Greek scales. There followed *Barstow* and *Daphne of the Dunes*. After that was heard *Castor and Pollux*, which the composer described as "a dance for the twin rhythms of Gemini." (This work should, of course, not be confused with the seventeenth-century opera of the same name by the French master, Rameau.) Also heard were *And on the Seventh Day the Petals Fell in Petaluma; Exordium;* and *Delusion and Fury*, subtitled "a ritual of dream and delusion."

"It was plain," reported Theodore Strongin in *The New York Times*, "that Mr. Partch is fanciful, whimsical, and a philosopher. . . . It was even plainer . . . that in the best sense he has never grown up. *Petals* and *Exordium* in particular have a kind of wide-eyed simplicity, a lack of disillusion, that is unaffected by the oversophisticated Western musical practices." Strongin said about *Petals:* "Each episode seemed a segment of some far-off continuous music that reveals itself to us only at moment of hearing. It is an amiable, even funny piece." As for *Exordium*, "the sounds slid around one another in angular but very listenable patterns." Donald Henahan, in describing *Daphne of the Dunes* and *Castor and Pollux* wrote: "The mingling sonorities . . . evoke music of the Orient, the South Seas, the American Indian and other non-European traditions."

No less a distinguished musicologist than Jacques Barzun, professor of music at Columbia University and the author of a distinguished biography of Berlioz, has called Partch's musical-dramatic writing as "the most original and powerful contribution to dramatic music on the continent. These musical-dramatic works are a compromise between drama and a masque, a form he has designed as "satyr-play music for the dance theater" ("satura," a Roman word meaning "medley" from which we have derived the word "satire"). One such satyr-play is *Ring Around the Moon*, described by Partch as "a satire on the world of singers and singing, music and dance, on concert and concert audiences." He also regarded it as a "satire on the world in general, on whimsy and caprice . . . on grand flourishes that lead to nothing, on satyrs, or on nothing." *Ring Around the Moon* is the third part of a trilogy, the other two being the previously mentioned *Castor and Pollux* and *Even Wild Horses* in which excerpts from Rimbaud's *A Season in Hell* are declaimed.

Within this musico-dramatic category is Partch's setting of William Butler Yeats' translation of Sophocles' *Oedipus Rex (King Oedipus)*. Partch created neither a play with incidental music nor an opera, but a concert work for actors and instruments, with the speaking parts assigned by the composer the precise tone, inflection, and rhythm. This work was originally written in Partch's microtonal style, but because of the difficulty of gathering a cast of singers and instrumentalists capable of performing such music, Partch had to compromise and translate his microtonal score into the traditional scales, though considerable gliding from one note to another and glissandi continually give the impression of microtonal music.

Here is what Partch himself has said about *King Oedipus:* "The music is conceived as an emotional saturation that is the particular of dramatic music to achieve. My idea has been to present the drama expressed by the language, not to obscure it, whether by operatic aria or symphonic instrumentation. Hence in critical dialogue, music enters almost insidiously as tensions enter." Discussing Partch's treatment of *Oedipus Rex,* the distinguished critic, Alfred Frankenstein, said that "the score vastly enhanced the ominous tension of the tragedy."

The Bewitched (about which we spoke earlier) also belongs with his musico-dramatic compositions. So is a work that was completed early in the 1960s: *Water! Water!,* comprising eleven prologues and nine epilogues separated by an intermission. There is a slender theme running like a thread through this work which highlights the futile struggle of man to control nature. The control of nature is symbolized by a city dam. Nature's victory is suggested by the floods that destroy the dam and the city. Partch here divided the stage into two sections. One is an American city (Santa Mystiana), populated by an alderman, disk jockey, lady mayor, and baseball commentator among others; the second is an open countryside.

Water! Water! was followed by another musico-dramatic composition called *Revelation in Courthouse Park.* Greek mythology here is once again the source of Partch's subject matter: specifically, Euripides' *Bacchae*. But ancient Thebes becomes a modern American park, and ancient Dionysius is transformed into a Hollywood star, Dion. Much of the music is discordant, played on Partchian instruments; much of it is also satirical, often parodying "pop" tunes.

Whether Partch is as important as his retinue of ardent admirers maintain, or as inconsequential as some of his severest critics believe him to be, he *has* contributed something new and exciting to our new music. Partch may be discounted or laughed at, which is often the case. But he cannot be ignored. Will Partch be today's Charles Ives—a composer who half a century from now will be looked upon as a visionary who had had a glimpse into music's future? Will Partch's cumbersome microtonal scale and his unique instruments of his own invention (as well as his highly personal ideas and concepts about music) provide some of the threads from which the fabric of the music of tomorrow will be woven? These questions will some day get their reply. Meanwhile, we are the beneficiaries of a good deal of novel, refreshing, sometimes exciting, often highly imaginative musical adventures—if we stand ready and willing to follow the advice of Charles Ives' father to stretch our ears and our imagination.

Index